DHAMMAPADA

Dedicated

to

Lord Buddha

In search of Truth O Shakya! more than
two thousand five hundred years ago,
you came to Bodh-Gaya and you sat
in a lotus position under the Bodhi tree, and
attained the Enlightenment

Men in the present world are guided by
negative thinking which results in
destruction, killing, hatred and
all sorts of malpractices

O Lord! Our teacher! O great emancipator of the world!
we need you more today and
pray to come again on the earth

Lord Buddha

Most sacred Mahabodhi Temple where Bhagavana Buddha attained Enlightenment.

DHAMMAPADA

MAHESH KUMAR SHARAN

ABHINAV PUBLICATIONS

abhinav publications

Cataloging in Publication Data—DK
Courtesy: D.K. Agencies (P) Ltd. <docinfo@dkagencies.com>

Sharan, Mahesh Kumar.
Dhammapada / Mahesh Kumar Sharan.
p. cm.
Text in Pali (roman); translation, explanation and introductory matter in English. Includes bibliographical references (p.)

ISBN 8170174759

1. Buddhism—Sacred books—Early works to 1800. 2. Buddhism—Doctrines. 3. Philosophy, Buddhist.
I. Tripitaka. Suttanipitaka. Khuddakanikaya. Dhammapada. English & Pali. II. Title.

DDC 294.382 22

First Published in India 2006

Publishers
Shakti Malik
Abhinav Publications
E-37 Hauz Khas
New Delhi-110016 (INDIA)
Phones: 26566387, 26562784, 26524658
Fax: 91-11-26857009
e-mail: shakti@nde.vsnl.net.in
website: http://www.abhinavexports.com

ISBN 81-7017-475-9

Phototypesetting and processing by
Onkar Digital Studio, Rohini, Delhi

Printed at
D.K. Fine Art Press P. Ltd., Ashok Vihar, Delhi

CONTENTS

FOREWORD

Dhammapada is the most beautiful compendium of Buddhist thought and philosophy. The present work has been accomplished by Dr. Mahesh Kumar Sharan, erudite Professor and Head of the Post-Graduate Department of Ancient Indian and Asian Studies, Gaya College, Gaya. It is a wonderful work critically analysing and discussing the theme of the *Dhammapada* in its manifold dimensions.

The book lends itself readily to an indepth study of this religious classic of mankind to the great delight of scholars and the students both.

From the study of the *Dhammapada* one can learn the fundamental teachings and also the elements of Buddhist way of life. It will lead a reader not only to a happy and prosperous life here and hereafter but also to the achievement of life's purpose—the highest goal of life and bliss.

It is my humble desire that the *Dhammapada* may prove to be a beacon of light guiding the present human population of the world as also the future generations. The book may be a constant companion to all guiding and leading everybody to righteousness and virtue towards the ultimate goal of total bliss.

In my opinion the book honestly translated and edited by Dr. Sharan will prove to be the most useful work and treatise for all scholars of philosophy, teachings and learning.

I bless Dr. Sharan for his long life so that he may

bring out some more sacred and valuable books for orientation of a holy life of all human beings.

I have no doubt that his painstaking and scholarly work will receive due appreciation from the learned scholars on Buddhism of India and abroad.

Dr. Braj Mohan Pandey 'Nalin'
President
Indian Congress of Pali and Buddhist Studies and former University Professor and Head of the Department of Pali and Prakrit, Magadh University, Bodh Gaya and Visiting Professor
Nava Nalanda Mahavihar, Nalanda (Bihar)

MESSAGES ON BUDDHA

HIS HOLINESS THE LORD ABBOT WAT THAI, BODH GAYA

The publication of the *Dhammapada* by Dr. Mahesh Kumar Sharan—a reputed scholar in the field of Indology, is a welcome edition for the propagation of the teachings of the Lord Buddha. I congratulate Dr. Sharan for this scholarly work which is the product of his painstaking research.

The *Dhammapada* presents a practical manual and guide to those who seek to realise *Nibbāna.* Its terse sayings in Pali verse on a variety of subjects range from happiness, anger and craving to enlightenment. These verses, memorised by young monks and lay-believers of all ages across the world, embody the very spirit of the Buddha's teachings.

May the present publication prove to be an important milestone in extending world peace since the teachings of the Lord are for the benefit of entire mankind. Also, it will go a long way in removing the feeling of hatred and tension and jealousy among the people. The universe is one, the humanity is one and the key to open it is also one. Here lies the greatness of Buddhism with the message of peace, amity, prosperity and universalism.

Sab be satta sukhi hontu
Sarve bhavantu sukhinah.

Let all mankind be happy.

Dr. Phra Raj Bodhivides
M.A., Ph.D.

PRESIDENT-CUM-MEDITATION TEACHER, INTERNATIONAL MEDITATION CENTRE, BODH GAYA

Buddhism is a religion that prescribes certain ways of living with ethical and psychological codes of conduct and behaviours. This is a personal system of mind purification, mind training and mind transformation.

The Buddha's philosophy is the cream of Indian social values, culture and civilisation. The religion is for the promotion of social happiness and prosperity. Therefore, Buddhism as the most rational and pragmatic religion aims at the promotion of all varied zests and interests of life values in the society. It teaches how the individual and social life can be best led as the Enlightened life, carefree, detached and released life with full farsights and insights.

In spite of innumerable works by eminent thinkers and scholars on *Dhammapada,* it is so encyclopaedic in character that many aspects of it are yet to be studied and understood. Dr. Mahesh Kumar Sharan's approach is entirely new and his explanations are bound to invite the attention of scholars. I have no doubt that scholars and laymen will read this work with great interest and pleasure.

Saddhim hontu sukhi sabbe, parivaehi attano,
Anigha sumana hontu saha sabbehi natibhi.

May all enjoy happiness along with their family. May all enjoy undisturbed peace and pleasant-mindedness with all their kith and kin.

Ven. Dr. Rastrapal Mahathera
M.A., Ph.D., Tripitaka Visarada

DISTRICT MAGISTRATE, GAYA

Loving kindness (*Metta*), compassion (*Karuṇa*) and altruistic joy (*Mudita*) and sharing the difficulties of others is the message of Lord Buddha which should be practised by all to keep the world in order. Individuals and nations should cultivate good and avoid evil. If individuals and nations are pure and unselfish in mind, actions and speech, happiness will follow them. In this world hatred is never cured by hatred, hatred can only be cured by love. This is the eternal love which is conducive to the growth of happiness. People and nations should not desire success by unjust means like fighting, quarrelling or by war.

Dr. M.K. Sharan's translation and explanations on *Dhammapada* is a welcome edition. He has worked with commendable patience and devotion and has published this book that would help in understanding Lord Buddha's teachings on human suffering. All the verses of the text are fine, beautiful, and melodious. Through these verses, the Buddha exhorts one to achieve the greatest of all conquests—the conquest of self, to escape from the evils of passion, hatred and ignorance and to strive hard to attain freedom from the cycle of rebirth i.e. the way to *Nirvāṇa.*

I have great pleasure in congratulating Dr. Sharan on this very useful book.

Chaitanya Prasad
District Magistrate &
Collector-cum-Chairman
Bodh Gaya Temple Management Committee
Bodh Gaya

RABINDRANATH TAGORE

The world today is wild with the delirium of hatred, the conflicts are cruel and unceasing in anguish, crooked are its paths, tangled its bonds of greed.

All creatures are crying for a new birth of thine,
Oh thou of boundless life,
save them, rouse thine eternal voice of hope,
let Love's lotus with its inexhaustible treasure of honey open its petals in thy light.
O Serene, O Free,
in thine immeasurable mercy and goodness wipe away all dark stains from the heart of this earth.
Thou giver of immortal gifts
give us the power of renunciation
and claim from us our pride,
In the splendour of a new sunrise of wisdom
Let the blind gain their sight
and let life come to the souls that are dead,
O Serene, O Free,
in thine immeasurable mercy and goodness wipe away all dark stains from the heart of this earth.
Man's heart is anguished with the fever of unrest
with the poison of self-seeking,
with a thirst that knows no end.
Countries far and wide flaunt on their
foreheads the blood-red mark of hatred.
Touch them with the right hand,
make them one in spirit,

bring harmony into their life,
bring rhythm of beauty,
O Serene, O Free,
in thine immeasurable mercy and goodness wipe away all dark stains from the heart of this earth.

DR. S. RADHAKRISHNAN

We find in Gautama the Buddha, in powerful combination, spiritual profundity, moral strength of the highest order and a discreet intellectual reserve. He is one of those rare spirits who bring to men a realization of their own divinity and make the spiritual life seem adventurous and attractive, so that they may go forth into the world with a new interest and a new joy at heart. While his great intellect and wisdom gave him comprehension of the highest truth, his warm heart led him to devote his life to save from sorrow suffering humanity, thus confirming the great mystic tradition that true immortals occupy themselves with human affairs, even though they possess divine souls. The greatness of his personality, his prophetic zeal and burning love for suffering humanity, made a deep impression on those with whom he lived. His true greatness stands out clearer and brighter as the ages pass and even the sceptical-minded are turning to him with a more real appreciation, a deeper reverence and a truer worship. He is one of those few heroes of humanity who have made epochs to the history of our race, with a message for other times as well as their own.

The Second President of India
and a great scholar of Indian
Philosophy, Ethics and
Thinker of modern India

PT. JAWAHARLAL NEHRU

(1)

The conception of the Buddha, to which innumerable loving hands have given shape in carven stone and marble and bronze, seems to symbolise the whole spirit of Indian thought, or at least one vital aspect of it. Seated on the lotus flower, calm and impassive above passion and desire, beyond the storm and strife of this world, so far away he seems out of reach, unattainable. Yet again we look and behind those still unmoving features there is a passion and an emotion, strange and more powerful than the passions and emotions we have known. His eyes are closed, but some power of the spirit looks out of them and a vital energy fills the frame. The ages roll by and Buddha seems not so far away after all; his voice whispers in our ears and tells us not to run away from the struggle, but, calm eyed, to face it, and to see in life ever greater opportunities of growth and advancement.

(The First Prime Minister of India)
—On the occasion of the opening
of the Sanchi Vihara, November 1952)

(2)

We live in an age of conflict and war, of hatred and violence, all over the world. Never before has the need been the greater for all of us to remember that immortal message which Lord Buddha, the greatest and noblest of the sons of India, gave to us, and to you, and to all the world. That message of two thousand five hundred years ago is a living message today enshrined in our hearts and we draw inspiration from it to face the troubles and difficulties that threaten to overwhelm us.

—On the occasion of
2500th Buddha Birth Anniversary, 1956

PREFACE

Lord Buddha's doctrine was based on the ideals of love and charity, compassion and wisdom, purity and morality, self-restraint and the elimination of passions and desires. The light and guidance of the Lord's teachings and rededication to the ideals of *Ahimsa*, *Karuna* and *Seva* are essential for the welfare and happiness of humanity today. Now is the time more necessary, more requisite and more essential to spread the message of peace, the gospel of loving kindness as expounded by Lord Buddha, all over the world. So we have to be united in one movement and take and go forward hand in hand to propagate this holy gospel, which is not only our greatest duty but also fulfilling the aspirations of the Lord.

Buddhism is a way of life by the enlightened one for the liberation of man from the suffering. This religion is a great virtue and is useful for peaceful co-existence among nations in every country with any race in the eye of muddle, where tensions exist overwhelmingly on all sides.

Bodh Gaya has been the centre of religious and cultural activities since time immemorial. Buddha underwent renunciation (*Pabajja*) when he was 29. After leaving his home at Kapilavastu, Buddha spent some time at Rajgir and subsequently devoted much of his time at Bodh Gaya (formerly Uruvela) in search of peace, where he could meditate under a *Peepal* tree. After living rigorous ascetic life for about six years here he attained Enlightenment. And it was here that in the seventh week since his Enlightenment he determined to start the world mission through his religion—Buddhism. Bodh Gaya being the most famous and holiest place for the Buddhists in the world, we expect more pilgrims and tourists every year to come to this holiest place to get rid of renunciation (*Nibbāna*) according to the Lord. It is the best and most suitable place for the work of the propagation of Buddha's teachings in the most successful way, a permanent rendezvous for Buddhists all over the world to meet and discuss service to their religion.

The purpose of establishing the International Buddhist Brotherhood Association in Japanese Temple at Bodh Gaya in the year 1972 was to unite the Buddhists of all countries for the propagation and practice which binds man to the highest goal for the benefit of every human being. In the first week of December every year a seminar for two days is held in the Japanese Temple and participants from Buddhist countries attend the seminar.

In order to commemorate the journey of peace started by the Lord, we have been successfully organising the *Buddha Mahotsava* since 1998. Being a teacher of the Magadh University Bodh Gaya posted in Gaya College in the Post-Graduate Department of Ancient Indian and Asian Studies, I am associated with all activities and programmes and also I am one of the members of the Editorial Board of the Souvenir *Buddha Vandana* since 1999 which is published on this occasion. For one day seminar is also conducted. The celebration of the *Buddha Mahotsava* every year with great sincerity is of utmost significance from the cultural, economic, social and political perspectives apart from its puritan religious aspects. Bodh Gaya formally and deservedly has been inscribed on the world heritage list of the UNESCO on June 24, 2002.

Dhammapada is the most important compendium of Buddhist anthology—a collection of verses which are endowed with humanistic manifestations. It has the same place in Buddhism as the *Gita* in Hinduism. It is one of the texts grouped under *Khuddaka Nikaya.* Though this book is the smallest of the group in size, its importance can by no means be lessened, since it contains the essence of the teachings of the Buddha compiled in the *Tripitaka* Buddhist scriptures. Although there exist various English translations of the *Dhammapada* such as *The Footsteps of Religion, A Collection of Verses, Sentences of Religion, Verses on Dhamma, The Word of Buddha,* and *The Path of Virtue,* the main purpose of publishing the *Dhammapada* is to spread the teachings of the Lord which is most needed in the present materialistic world.

We are passing through a very deplorable situation hence we have to think about our existence. According to Buddhist view of life there is no method of relief to the world other than Buddhism.

I feel this is the opportune moment for all to proclaim the great compassion of Gautama Buddha so that the world peace and welfare of all mankind be promoted not only spiritually but socially and economically also.

The teachings of *Dhammapada* (*Sukkhavagga*) such as "conqueror breeds hatred, vanquished lies in pain; the peaceful one lies happily giving up both victory and defeat", which taught the ambitious conquerors like the Mauryan King Asoka to lay down arms and to devote the energy and wealth, which used to be employed for the destruction and misery of mankind, for its welfare and happiness, are the greatest need of even the so-called civilized world.

In this look I have given the original *Pali* texts in Roman script along with the translation for the use of the readers who wish to make a deeper study. In making this translation I have consulted several translations of the *Dhammapada* of which I must specially mention with thankfulness the translations of Ven. Narain Thera, Prof. N.K. Bhagawat, Ven. U. Dhammajoti and Shri Silananda Brahmachari.

I must express my indebtedness to Shri Vidya Sagar Gupta, A.D.M. (Retd.), a doyen of philosophers, for making many valuable suggestions. I am also greatly indebted to my eldest brother Dr. Awadhesh Kumar Sharan who very carefully read the manuscript in the beginning and improved it.

My thanks are also due to the great scholars in the field from whose works I have benefited much in my present work. As regards the views, interpretations and opinions expressed in the present work as well as their shortcomings, the responsibility is entirely mine.

I am indebted to Dr. Braj Mohan Pandey 'Nalin', M.A. (Sanskrit, Hindi, Pali, Gold Medallist), Ph.D., D.Litt., former Prof. & Head, Deptt. of Pali and Prakrit, Magadh University, Bodh Gaya for his proffered advice and information and without whose constant assistance, guidance and encouragement, this work would not have been possible. Moreover, he has laid me under deep obligation by contributing Foreword to this volume.

My thanks are also due to my wife Dr. (Smt.) Nirmala Sharan, who as usual kept me aloof from the household affairs and left me free to go on with my work. It is difficult to express my deep sense of gratitude to my daughter Dr. (Smt.) Manisha Sharan, my son Manish Kumar Sharan, sister Smt. Manjula

Sharan, brother-in-law Shri Hari Narayan Prasad, son-in-law Shri Rajesh Prasad and my colleague Dr. Rajan Gupta who helped me with their valuable suggestions and encouragements.

The labour taken will be justified if this publication proves useful to the readers.

I pray that Lord Buddha's shining light may guide us on the path of *Dhamma.*

Bhavatu Sabba Mangalam.

May all be happy and serene.

June 30, 2005 **Mahesh Kumar Sharan**
Aparajita
Magadh Colony, Gaya

INTRODUCTION

Buddha was born on a full-moon day in the year 563 B.C. His father King *Śuddhodana* was ruler of princely state of Kapilavastu situated in the foothills of Nepal. His mother, *Mahāmāyā,* was on her way to her parents' house to deliver a child in a chariot when on the way she felt pain and delivered the prince under a *Shaal* tree in the royal *Lumbini* grove. Mother *Mahāmāyā* expired when the prince was only seven days old. The responsibility of bringing him up was entrusted to the child's step-mother *Prajapati Gautami* who happened to be the sister of his mother.

The child was named *Siddhartha* during his early age and his family name was *Gautama.* Father *Śuddhodana* belonged to the ruling clan of the *Sakyas.* *Siddhartha* (*Gautama*) was married at the age of 16 to a princess named *Yasodhara.* She was beautiful and devoted. The couple lived in their palace at *Kapilavastu* and led a luxurious life. King *Śuddhodana* kept his son away from the sight of any suffering humanity but the prince happened to observe old age, limping lames and the dead during his princely strolls outside his palace and became deeply moved at such sights of sufferings. *Siddhartha* made a determination to find the cause of such sufferings and to discover the way out from these universal phenomena and, as such, in quest of solutions he left his kingdom, his loving wife *Yasodhara* and an infant child—*Rahula* while the lady and the child were asleep. This happened when *Gautama's* age was 29. *Rahula* was very small. *Gautama* disrobed himself from princely dress and adopted the appearance of ascetics in search of the solution—human sufferings, their causes and how to get rid of them.

In dense forests *Siddhartha* remained loitering for six years. He met quite a good number of religious teachers of that time. Discourses rendered by them could not quench his thirst of genuine solution. He resorted to various penances and self-mortification. He studied various doctrines and remained in association of disciples of religious personalities but they failed to satisfy *Gautama.*

Wandering ahead he came to *Uruvela* near present-day Bodh Gaya situated at a distance of seven miles south of Gaya in the state of Bihar. This village was situated on the west bank of river *Niranjana.* Finding a suitable place like *Uruvela* he practised severe austerities without taking any food or water. His body turned into a skeleton. It was here, at *Uruvela,* that *Gautama* attained Enlightenment. And from this day of attainment *Gautama* became metamorphosed into Lord Buddha—"The Enlightened". He founded Buddhism.

At *Saranath* near today's *Varanasi* in Uttar Pradesh he delivered his first sermon and thereafter continuously for 45 years he taught all classes of people without any consideration of their status, caste and creed. Listeners of his sermons and preachings were Rulers, Brahmins, farmers, outcastes, beggars, religious men and even robbers and thieves. Buddha did not make any distinction between them.

The most outstanding event in the sixth century B.C. is the emergence of Buddhism, preached by the Buddha—the Enlightened. He is considered to be the first historic figure in Indian civilisation to conceive the fundamental unity of all beings and to give effective expression to a feeling that humanity has a common bond and a common end. The messages of this great Master and humanitarian—the doctrine of unity and universal brotherhood of man, though frequently quoted and sound laudable, yet the concept thereof was undoubtedly unthinkable in the extreme at a time of more than two thousand five hundred years ago.

Buddhism played a great role in building the culture and history of India and for ages it continued to influence the heart, mind and action of the Indian people. It gave a new philosophy of life, a new message of hope and a happy goal that every individual can attain through his personal efforts. It is still a great force and its magnetic charm and influence is still irresistible. This is why it has so many adherents in different parts of the world and the number of its followers in the land of its origin is also on the increase.

Buddha has taught us to behave as good neighbours, treating others with an equal and impartial eye. If there are lapses they will have to be set right as soon as possible. A verse in *Dhammapada* says that Buddha tells the way and that each one of us has to swelter at the task. It is not the question of merely listening to the advice and going home and sleeping over it, but it is something which costs enormous effort if we are true Buddhists. So far as our practice is concerned Buddha showed the path, indicated the direction, told us what we should do but the effort should be the individual's own.

The teachings of Buddha are known as the "Middle Path". They are a golden mean between the two extremes, because they avoid both the extremities of a thoughtless luxurious life and a cruel torture of penance. He taught people the great importance of moderation and a middle path in social life. The value of love, kindness and truth as means to achieve peace and order was brought home to the people, and social service, education and morality were given more importance than power and position. The simplicity of his teachings, the abolition of cumbersome rites and rituals, the democratic essence of his doctrine and the emphasis on peace and tranquillity in individual and social life attracted the people towards Buddhism. Also his dynamic personality and his serenely peaceful composure were greatly responsible for the unprecedented rise of Buddhism at home and abroad.

Buddha's teachings are universal in essence and when practised sincerely and *ab imo pectore* by the leaders, diplomats and statesmen, can guarantee us the eagerly desired international understanding and world peace. An honest application of the Four Noble Truths and of the Eightfold Path in national and international policies, plans and politics can ensure mankind world peace. The principles of mutual respect for each nation's territorial integrity and sovereignty, mutual non-aggression, mutual non-interference in each other's internal affairs, equality and mutual benefits and peaceful co-existence among nations embodied in the *Panchasheel* advocated by India's creative mind can be realised effectively through the teachings of Buddha. Our constant refrain in all national and international forums and agencies should be: "Through Buddhism the World Peace".

Thus, Buddhism can be a powerful source of world peace and of international understanding among nations. We can discern several points of contact between the current political ideologies and the Buddhist doctrine as propounded by its founder. It would be worthwhile to investigate the relation between the two in the context of world peace and fellowship among nations.

From the study of Buddha's social egalitarianism and also from his principle of decentralization of authority in the *Sangha*, it may be inferred that democracy, a Government of the people, by the people and for the people, would be much in accordance and agreement with his teachings. Though an aristocrat by birth, he was a democrat.

Chronologically viewed, Buddha's teachings are more than 2500 years old, but they are quite fresh and relevant even today. Far from being outdated and forgotten in the limbo of the past, they twinkle in the political horizon of the nations in a never-ending milky way. Buddhist democracies, geographically big or small, located in different latitudes and longitudes can usher in the age of world peace and a new order of international harmony and cooperation on stable foundations.

As wars are born in the minds of men, peace, its powerful antidote, can also be planted in the same minds provided they are steadily nourished, nurtured and sustained by the universal principles of Buddhism which are hailed by great luminaries like Rainer Maria Rilke, John Masefield, T.S. Eliot, Edith Sitwell, Aldous Huxley, Bertrand Russel and others.

All this is not a mirage in the desert nor wishful thinking. World history records in its pages the glorious example of King Asoka of the Mauryan dynasty, who having turned over a new leaf after the memorable *Kalinga* campaign raised Buddhism to the status of world-religion and became a foremost representative of its teachings. They are presently very firmly rooted in Asian countries like Burma, Thailand, Cambodia, Vietnam, Tibet, China, Bali, Borneo, Sumatra, Java, Japan, Korea and in European countries like England, France and Germany. They are also taking their roots in several parts of America.

Asoka the Great universalised king boldly proclaimed the sound principles of international morality when he declared to the world that "the chiefest conquest is the conquest of Right and not of Might". He scrupulously respected the independence of all states, big as well as small. He despatched missions to them for the cultivation of the spirit of international reconciliation and world peace.

In our quest for world peace—Paz-Universal, the time-honoured doctrine of Buddhism can reshape our political thinking in terms of mankind, in terms of global understanding and of cosmic consciousness and in terms of a new social order and, through worldwide Buddhist education, usher in the much desired transformation of all Men and Nations leading to the Golden Age of World Peace.

Buddhism, being the practical religion of peace and non-violence, has to play a major role in guiding the destiny of mankind in this present crisis. Through Buddhism world peace can be eternally achieved and preserved without any danger to any life on this earth. Researches and foundations of Buddhism are most befitting to the present scientific age in which the spiritual or theological side is being completely neglected. The scientific outlooks and achievements of Buddhism, ever since its birth, are a standing challenge to some modern scientists devoid of human values. It has a scientific appeal, in terms of its pragmatic and experimental approach, and is ever ready to face all kinds of challenges by curbing the instructs of men away from the extremes and inducing them to move on to the right path, the middle way. Thus, Buddhism advises all men to take the right, balanced, consistent and harmonious approach as emerging from the natural thought process towards human welfare and progress. In its spectrum, there is no scope for hatred or violence of any kind. It was a built-in system for ensuring world peace. It offers love, compassion, balance and an ever increasing stream of higher evolution. Buddhism has the eternal radiance of hope in it through its cardinal message of peace and thereby it dispels the darkness of despair besetting our times.

One of the main reasons that nations wage war against each other and cannot live in peace and harmony is their lack of love and affection for their fellow men. The reason for this is that they are unable to see each other as close, appealing and valuable. Like Buddha all sentient beings are equally kind to us in contributing to peace, happiness and spiritual realisations and thus Buddhism teaches many ways to view sentient beings, to see them as having been our parents and to have the same respect for them that we have for our Teacher. Totally opposed to any form of violence which harms oneself or others, Buddhism teaches that one should practise what one preaches to others. Buddha set himself as a model before us and we must honestly try to live up to his expectations through thought and deeds to prove ourselves as worthy sons of a worthy father. *Buddha dharma* is an immaculate source of peace and happiness in the world, let us renew our sacred pledge to uphold the torch of peace handed down to the chain of teachers and sages from the Buddha to us.

The world today is on the brink of disaster. Violence, arms race, hatred and killing of innocent lives have vitiated the atmosphere of peace, harmony and brotherhood. Buddha's teachings are much more relevant today to bring sanity and love to guide human beings. Otherwise the future holds extreme danger to the globe. Universal brotherhood and love alone can save and sustain the world. It is time to rededicate ourselves to the path of Lord Buddha at this juncture. Poverty, illiteracy and hatred have raised roadblocks to the growth and prosperity of mankind. Poverty, hunger and insecurity must be banished and new order ushered in for bringing humanity back from the blind alley and grave danger staring at us. Human destination should be sublime. Strife and destruction is not our goal. Avarice, greed, ignorance, misunderstanding and hatred must be eradicated from human hearts.

Buddha's message of universalism can only unify mankind and bring about world peace. Buddhist wisdom can only save mankind from international cold war and confrontation and save itself from nuclear death and destruction.

Now we come to practical guidelines of Buddhism. Buddhism stresses on practising of moral virtues of friendliness (*Metta*), compassion (*Karuna*), altruistic joy in the happiness (*Mudita*) of others, equanimity (*Upekka*), charity (*Dana*), forbearance and fortitude and development of knowledge and wisdom. It is indeed a way of life which a Hindu, Sikh, Muslim and Christian can adopt in India. Humanism, kindness and consideration for fellow human beings and all living creatures, control and regulation of mind, development of one's self-thought, growth in knowledge and wisdom —all civilized persons anywhere in the world like to practise or to do.

In the quest for peace and happiness for mankind there can be no two opinions that man must be good. A good man can build up a good family. Several good families make a good community or society and the good people in the society make a good nation or country. Many good nations would make a good international community. A good man or good community or a good nation believes in co-existence and is not offensive or aggressive but sees his or its own faults or defects. The *Dhammapada* says "Speak not harshly to anyone: Those thus addressed will retort: Painful indeed is vindictive speech. Exchanged blows may touch you" (*Dandavagga,* 5).

A good man is also not fault finding. The *Dhammapada* says, "He should not regard the faults of others, things done and left undone by others but his own deeds done and undone" (*Pupphavagga,* 7).

His mind is full of love and compassion for other human beings, for animals and other living creatures. He is friendly to everybody and desires good for all and prays for saving all from evil. He feels happy when others are happy and prosperous and is not jealous of them. Even though his endeavour is to do good to others, if others try to harm him, he does not think of reprisal or revenge. He does not strike nor cause to strike others comparing others with oneself (*Sahassavagga,* 2).

He is more interested in conquering himself rather than conquering others (*Sahassavagga,* 4-5).

He believes that hatred never ceases by hatred in this world (*Yamakavagga,* 5).

His mind is free from ignorance, lust, greed or hatred. Instead of these negative traits or qualities (*Akusala*) he believes and practises the positive virtues of compassion and love. He does not believe in quarrels because in quarrels men perish (*Yamakavagga,* 6).

He does not steal, he does not take intoxicating drinks, he does not kill, he does not indulge in adultery and he does not lie. He is thoughtful and meditative and is aware of the evil consequences of the different taints and wrongful behaviour.

Buddhism desires that individuals and communities should have a high moral life and high idealism and try to transcend the narrow "self" because in ultimate analysis the small and narrow separate self does not exist. Only when the individuals know this and are just, righteous, truthful, charitable and compassionate and violence and hatred are abjured, there can be a peaceful and happy world.

Buddha's teachings in their essential and formal aspects were of universal application based on equality of men and were not for any particular caste or class or for any particular nation or particular age. His teachings were meant not only for the *Bhikkhus* or aspirants of 'Brahminhood' but even for ordinary lay men or women, the rich and the poor, the learned and the so-called 'unlearned', the preacher and non-preacher, they all could strive for being better and ultimately the "perfect" human beings. The door to *Nirvana* was open to all, provided efforts were made to reach that door. Kindness to fellow-men and practice of truth and non-violence could be the trait of a very rich man as well as the poorest labourer. No doubt, Buddha preached in India but his preachings and teachings were meant for all mankind of the world. He exhorted his disciples to go all over in different directions of the world with his message of peace and goodwill—*Bahujana hitaya* and *bahujana sukhaya*).

"Go Ye, O Bhikkhus and wander forth for the gain of the many, for the welfare of the many, in compassion for the world, for the good, for the gain, for the welfare of gods and men. Proclaim, O Bhikkhus, the Doctrine glorious, preach ye a life of holiness, perfect and pure."

(*Mahavagga, Vinayapitaka*)

DHAMMAPADA ON PRACTICE OF BUDDHISM

Although man seeks a peaceful and contented happy life, he has not taken care to adopt the proper ways and means to attain them. He tries to have a short-cut to a congenial situation for which he continuously struggles, many a time vainly. Being urged by the desire he dreams and struggles hard and when he is unsuccessful in his attempts he resigns to his lot and considers his failures as the dictates of destiny or nature. And as such man has remained helplessly drifting from one orientation to the other thereby dislocating himself without a purpose.

We have to improve the quality of life and make it objective-oriented in order to make life meaningful and significant. We shall have to know whence and why we have come and where do we go in the end. Relationships among human beings are unsatisfactory. In economic, political, social, intellectual and even religious and public life tensions are becoming almost universal. Unsatisfactoriness of our living is apparent and the quality of life seems to be going down from worse to worst everywhere in the world. Nobody is happy with whatever he has achieved. Human mind is not at peace or rest in this milieu and even the peace and happiness that we get, are not permanent. Life is uncertain at present. Nobody can say for tomorrow. We have to imagine how we can get lasting peace and happiness? How would we improve the quality of life and make it purposeful? How Buddhism will help us? How does Buddhism—a living religion of the world today, in our everyday life help us in this matter? Religion to help us must also be made a duly practice by all people, old and young, the intelligentsia or the common people.

Of the 26 *vaggas* or chapters of the *Dhammapada* seven chapters—*Appamādavagga, Pāpavagga, Sukkhavagga, Piyavagga, Kodhavagga, Malavagga* and *Taṇhāvagga* refer to the qualities of heedfulness of means of achieving happiness and the need for avoiding unheedfulness (*pamada*), evil (*papa*), anger (*krodha*), impurities (*mala*), and craving (*tala*) and to develop affection (*piya*) as a universal prescription for mankind irrespective of one being young or old, a householder or a monk.

In verse 1 of *Jarāvagga* (old age) it is stated—when the world is ever ablaze, what is there to laugh or to be joyous about? Covered by the darkness why do you not seek the light?

It further states in verse 7 of the same *vagga* that the man of little learning grows old like a bull, his flesh increases but not his wisdom.

Verses 9 and 10 of the same *vagga* emphasise the need for leading a holy life *Brahmacharya* and say that those who have not led the holy life or have not obtained spiritual wealth (*Dhanam*), pine away like old herons on a pond without fish or lie, like worn-out bows, sighing after the past.

Among the *grihasthas* (householders), there are the *panditas* (wise), the just or the righteous (*Dhammatha*) and fools (*bala*), and amongst the monks there are the *Bhikkhus,* and the *Samanas* and for all of them the path of the Enlightened One is indicated in the *Buddhavagga.* Householders may belong to different professions, may be students, lecturers, labourers, business executives, public servants and even ministers, they may belong to any age group—young, middle-aged and old but all these will not preclude them from following the path of truth, purity, lustlessness, angerlessness, impuritylessness, hatredlessness, heedlessness, and evillessness and practise the positive virtues of love, compassion, affection and altruism. Adherence to such virtues and truths makes a person, a student, a labourer, an executive, a government employee and a minister conscious of his duty. If these virtues are practised all round, there would be less of confrontation and conflict and more of cordiality and concord, sympathy and understanding will develop and help us.

Exploitation of one-another will cease. There will be less of student strike, strike by labour and lockout of factories by management. Everyone in his profession will give his best and also will get his best in return. Hence, many of our social, economic and political problems can get resolved. The *Dhammapada* tells us to be actively detached or detachedly active. In life, many a time, one finds a difficult person to deal with. There are fools and evil minded persons. Verse 3 of *Paṇḍitavagga* says that do not associate with evil friends and do not associate with those who are mean. Associate only with righteous friends and associate with those who are noble.

Hence, according to *Dhammapada* we have to deal with them with a pure and developed mind which also understands his mind. If there is anger in his mind, he has to be met with non-anger. If he has hatred, he has to be met with non-hatred. If anger is met with anger and hatred with hatred, there is no end to them. Verse 5 of *Yamakavagga* says, for, in this world, hatreds never cease by hatred, hatreds cease only by love. This is the eternal law. "One should not be vindictive in body, mind and speech." Verse 5 of *Daṇḍavagga* says, speak not harshly to anyone, those thus spoken to may retort, vindictive speech is indeed painful and blows may be returned to you for blows. In verse 7 of *Arahantavagga* we read his mind is calm, his word is calm and his deed is calm, who, rightly knowing, is wholly freed and perfectly peaceful. In verse 9 of *Paṇḍitavagga* it is stated that one should not wish one's own prosperity by unfair means. In verse 7 of *Buddhavagga*, the advice of the Enlightened One is said to be not to insult and not to harm others. Many a time we think and talk in terms of victory and defeat. Verse 5 of *Sukkhavagga* says—A sage with calm mind lives happily beyond the domain of victory and defeat.

Now we come back to tensions and conflicts. These generally cause lack of peace and happiness. In summary we find that tensions and conflicts arise out of desire, craving and attachment. We can shed desire, craving and attachment if we understand the true nature of things and life. After having this understanding, we realise that tensions and conflicts can be reduced or done away with only when we control our body and mind. Control of body may be achieved by controlling the senses of sight, touch, smell, hearing and taste and organs like hands and feet. Regulation of the senses and use of the organs help in getting a 'healthy' body and 'healthy' mind. For regulation of mind, what is necessary is to have right thought and observance of an ethical code of conduct. Just as the mind can be made pure by cleansing process of good and right thought, the body has also to be kept clean and sustained with wholesome and nutritive thought. Nutrition is essential both for mind and body. The *Dhammapada* gives us an insight into the mysterious and true nature of life and existence and indicates how we get bogged down in the morass of attachment, craving and desire.

In *Bālavagga* verse 3, we find mention about attachment in this way "There are my sons, there is my wealth, thus worries the fool. He himself is not his own what to speak of sons and wealth?"

Maggavagga verse 15 lays stress on such a deeply attached person who is overwhelmed with thoughts on children and wealth, is snatched away by death like the sleeping village (washed away) by the great flood. Verse 16 says, neither son nor father nor friends stand to save. There is no protection from kinsmen for one at the jaws of death. Having realised this fact a wise one restrained morally clears the way to *Nibbāna* expeditiously.

Verse 12 of *Taṇhāvagga* says that the wise do not call a bond strong that is made of iron, wood or hemp, the attachment for jewels and ornaments, children and wives.

In verse 13 of *Pakiṇṇakavagga,* it is said that it is difficult to take delight in imperfect renunciation, painful is the life in houses where it is difficult to reside. The association with the unequal is painful. Suffering follows a wanderer. Therefore, let not a man be a wanderer (through births and deaths) and be followed by suffering.

Talking about attachment we find reference in verse 4 of *Pupphavagga* in the following manner. The man who gathers flowers (of sensual pleasures), whose mind is distracted, death carries him off as a great flood the sleeping village.

About the transience of body verses 2 and 3 of the *Jarāvagga* say—Behold this decorated body a mass of sores, erected (of bones), diseased, variously thought of, and which has no permanent standing. This worn-out body a nest of diseases is perishable, this foul body breaks up. Indeed the life ends in death.

In verse 4 of *Buddhavagga* it is mentioned that it is difficult to be born as a human being and to continue as such. In verse 8 it is mentioned that there is no satisfaction in sensual pleasures even by a shower of gold coins, sensual pleasures are of little relish and painful, knowing thus the wise men.

In verses 5-7 of *Maggavagga,* it is stated that when one perceives by insight that all conditioned things are transient, sorrowful and devoid of ego, one feels disgusted with the ills (of bodily existence). This itself is the way to purity.

When a man understands futility of attachment and transitoriness of things and life, the need for taking recourse to religion arises. Refuge i.e. faith and reverence to the Enlightened One and his teachings and also that of his monkhood i.e. religious life can only bring peace and happiness. Verses 12-14 of *Buddhavagga* say, "He who seeks refuge in the Buddha (Enlightened One), in the *Dhamma* (Doctrine), in the *Sangha* (Order), and with the right understanding sees the Four Noble Truths. The sorrow, the cause of sorrow, the cessation of sorrow, and the Noble Eightfold Path which leads to the cessation of sorrow. This refuge is secure indeed, this refuge is supreme, having come to this refuge, one is freed from all sufferings."

The Eightfold Path is the most important formula to lead holy life and one who observes it carefully with full attention becomes free from worldly cravenness and remains undisturbed by weal and woe and achieves the highest glory in life. This Eightfold Path prescribes a moral code of conduct after taking into account the reality or true nature of things and then an effort and investigation into truth by making the mind one-pointed through concentration. This path deals with ethical, spiritual and psychological aspects of life. In this path the right view has been propounded and established first. It is about the nature of the things of the world and it cannot be achieved without abandoning the belief in self. The belief in self is an ominous mental state which originates due to ignorance. And these ominous and inauspicious views are the fetters which bind the life of man. If one with firm determination and resolution wants to get rid of belief in self should acquire the knowledge of right views.

Dhammapada is most related with an individual who lives in this world, therefore humanistic values and virtues may be searched out in the Buddhist literature. It is endowed with meritorious virtues of humanity. Buddhism is a religion of applied humanity and knowledge.

Verses 19-20 of *Yamakavagga* emphasise the need for practical action after reading the sacred texts of religion—though a person recites much of the sacred texts, yet, if he, being negligent, does not live upto them, he will not share the holy life like the cowherd who counts the kine of others. Though a person recites very little from the sacred texts, but strictly follows the teachings and becomes fully enlightened with perfect freedom of mind throwing off lust, hatred and dullness, such one clinging to naught here and hereafter shares the blessings of monkhood.

The *Dhammapada* again emphasises the need of an individual's effort to practise religion in verses 4-5 and 9 of *Attavagga.* "For self is the master of self, who else could be the master? Having trained oneself well, one obtains the best master. By oneself alone is evil done, it is self-born and self-caused. Evil grinds the universe as a diamond, a hard gem. The evil done by one defiles oneself, not doing any evil one purifies oneself, one cannot purify another."

Verse 21 of *Bhikkhuvagga* says, "Self indeed is the saviour of self. Self indeed is one's refuge. Control, therefore, your own self as a merchant a noble stead."

Verse 6 of *Malavagga* says, "As the rust sprung from iron corrodes the same, having arisen from it, hence the transgressor is led to evil state by his own deeds."

A pragmatic religion like Buddhism when it asks one to practise it, it requires of him to know of the Five Aggregates (*Khanda*) viz. matter, feeling, perception, volitional activities and consciousness i.e. the functioning of body and mind. There is rise, growth and decay of mind and body of each individual. This fact can be constantly kept before us if we learn to meditate and discipline our body and mind i.e. practise *Yoga.* Thus also one learns to control desire and craving. Emphasis on meditation is in verse 10 of *Maggavagga*— indeed from meditation does wisdom spring, without meditation wisdom wanes.

Verse 21 of *Taṇhāvagga* says, "He who has destroyed craving overcomes all sorrows." Emphasis is on restraint and discipline in verse 2 of *Bhikkhuvagga*—good is restraint in body. Verse 3 refers to control of hand, foot and speech.

We are faced with the factor of chain-reaction in life— one cause is behind one effect, the effect as a cause is at the root of another effect and like that. If we understand the reality scientifically, it is easier for us to make our lives objective-oriented. The main objective is to know the purpose and meaning of life. Buddhism as a religion is objective-oriented. Its objective is to attain perfection or Enlightenment or *Nirvāṇa* after getting rid of imperfections and impediments to achieve this goal, but nevertheless striving: opportunity is given to us all, though only a few reach the summit. Verse 10 of *Paṇḍitavagga* says—There are only a few among men who go across. The rest of the people return to this very shore.

Enlightenment can be achieved only through spiritual and moral progress and the urge for it can arise only after development of mind and of wisdom. Only when a person is wise that he knows the need for self-control and the need to be peaceful just as a clear and still deep lake. We have to understand that attachment gives rise to sorrow, that he gives up attachment for everything. One is neither elated nor depressed by happiness or by pain. By developing right thought one has to give up sensual craving. Through insight into things light or enlightenment comes to him. He clears his mind of impurities and develops attentiveness and concentration. Thus mind becomes attentive and concentrated when the senses are controlled and it is made one-pointed as a measure of regular practice. Mind is ennobled by practising loving kindness (*Metta*), compassion (*Karuna*), altruistic joy as opposed to jealousy or envy (*Mudita*) and equanimity (*Upekkha*). Kindness, compassion, goodwill, altruism, etc. should first start in the family i.e. husband and wife, children and parents and then between relations, between neighbours, between social groups, between nations and nations.

In the proceedings of the 5th International Buddhist Conference held in the year 1979 by the International Buddhist Brotherhood Association, Japanese Temple, Bodh Gaya, Dr. A.K. Bandyopadhyay's article entitled *Practice of Buddhism in Day-to-day Life—Some Guidelines from the Dhammapada* is a research-oriented information for all. If one can practise on these guidelines, one has to win the battle against *Mara*. Faith, courage, conviction and determination are necessary to win the battle against *Mara*. Verse 5 of *Appamādavagga* of the *Dhammapada* says, "By effort, earnestness, discipline and self-control, let the wise man make for himself an island which no flood can overwhelm."

Before concluding the message of Lord Buddha through *Dhammapada*, it is worth noting a few words of Prof. Dr. Braj Mohan Pandey Nalin's learned article entitled "Human Value in Dhammapada" published in the *Buddha Vandana* on the occasion of *Buddha Mahotsava* held in the year 2000. He says, "Every human being should be sympathetic to one-another, because compassion and kindness has great importance among distressed persons. The meaning of distress is not that one is overpowered by disease but one who is captivated by greed, lust and jealousy. This is to say that without greed, lust and jealousy, one should lead one's life among greedy, lustful and jealous persons. This testifies that there can be no greater humanistic theories than all these put together. Thus it can be said without any hesitation that humanistic theory is fully engrained in *Dhammapada* like a pearl in a golden ring. Today, humanity is groping tremblingly in dread and darkness, in unrest and uncertainty as it did about two thousand and five hundred years ago. To root out the dread, to give the light, to tranquillise the mind and to assure humanity of physical and mental security persons with divine endowments will first do this work and none else. And time and space have proved that the great Lord Buddha's teachings have all the gradients to meet these needs. The teachings have found the most suitable place in *Dhammapada*. *Dhammapada* is nothing but collection of verses which are endowed with humanistic manifestations."

DHAMMAPADA

1. YAMAKAVAGGA
(TWIN)

1. Manopubbaṅgamā dhammā
manoseṭṭhā manomayā;
manasā ce paduṭṭhena
bhāsati vā karoti vā,
tato naṁ dukkhamanveti
cakkaṁ'va vahato padaṁ.

Mind precedes all mental states (*Dhamma*), mind is chief; they are mind-made. If with an impure mind a person speaks or acts then misery follows him like the wheel (of the chariot) follows the hoof of the beast of burden.

2. Manopubbaṅgamā dhammā
manoseṭṭhā manomayā;
manasā ce pasannena
bhāsati vā karoti vā,
tato naṁ sukkhamanveti
chāyā'va anapāyinī.

Mind precedes all mental states; mind is chief; they are mind-made. If with a pure mind, a person speaks or acts then happiness follows him like the shadow that never leaves.

Explanation 1-2

Indispensable are the results of *Karma* meaning action or deed, which follow the doer in this life or the life after. One's own *Karma* accounts for one's happiness or unhappiness. As the seed sown bears fruits, so a deed done yields its results. Needless to say, a good deed brings forth good results and bad deed bad results. Goodness or badness of *Karma* is dependent on the mind that acts behind the performance. A *Karma* is decidedly good when it is done with a good mind. It is bad when a bad mind runs the show.

It is clear that the mind goads one into performing an action. Otherwise, there is no performance of *Karma.* Mind or consciousness can play its part when the sense organs, such as eyes, ears etc. come in contact with their respective objects like sight, sound, etc. The mention of mind necessitates the mention of mental faculties also, which go to form the mind. These are nothing but elements of mind. In the above stanzas the word *Dhamma* means mental faculties. Because of its supremacy the mind leads all the mental faculties and excels them. Hence it is said that they are made of mind.

The mind is said to be bad or immoral when the immoral mental faculties like greed, hatred, envy, selfishness etc. defile, debase and degenerate the mind. If with such a mind one speaks or acts, suffering follows him as a consequence. Similarly, the mind is called good or undefiled when it is endowed with morally beautiful mental faculties. If such a mind elevated with piety and purity, love and devotion etc. manifests itself in the performance of *Karma,* happiness follows the doer as the result. Thus *Karma* becomes good or bad because of the mind behind and brings in happiness or miseries accordingly.

3. 'Akkocchi maṁ, avadhi maṁ,
ajini maṁ, ahāsi me,'
yeca taṁ upanayhanti,
veraṁ tesaṁ na sammati.

'He abused me, struck me, conquered me, robbed me,' those who cherish such thoughts, their hatred never appeases.

4. 'Akkocchi maṁ, avadhi maṁ,
ajini maṁ, ahāsi me,'
yeca taṁ nupanayhanti,
veraṁ tesūpasammati.

'He abused me, struck me, conquered me, robbed me,' those who do not cherish such thoughts their hatred appeases.

5. Na hi verena verāni
sammantīdha kudācanaṁ,
averena ca sammanti,
esa dhammo sanantano.

For, in this world, hatreds never cease by hatred, hatreds cease only by love. This is the eternal law.

Explanation 3-5

'Eye for eye' or 'tit for tat' is not a noble principle. Nor it solves the problem. Hatred begets hatred only. By entertaining it one not only does harm to others but to himself also, since it smoulders within like wild fire. It is not superfluous to say that hatred deluged the earth with blood more than once, reduced to ruins the cities and capitals and played havoc with the human society. Hatred can never conquer hatred. It is only love which can pacify it and ennoble the mind with heavenly feelings. The Compassionate One preached the lofty ideals of love to masses throughout His life.

6. Pare ca na vijānanti,
mayamettha yamāmase;
ye ca tattha vijānanti,
tato sammanti medhagā.

If the others do not realise (that the quarrels are bad), in this case let us restrain; there those who understand, from them the quarrels cease.

Explanation 6

When the veil of ignorance covers one's inner eyes, the life appears to him endless and the world a repository of pleasure. Such a person wastes away life in indulging in trivial matters without knowing that the world is transient and everything in the world comes into being just like bubbles in the running water only to get dissolved. One who views the world and life in their true perspective, finds no reason to indulge in strife.

7. Subhānupassiṁ viharantaṁ
indriyesu assaṁvutaṁ
bhojanamhi amattaññuṁ
kusītaṁ hīnavīriyaṁ,
taṁ ve pasahati Māro
vāto rukkhaṁ'va dubbalaṁ.

He who lives seeing pleasure (in the body), whose senses are uncontrolled, who is immoderate in food, is slothful and lacking in energy, *Māra* (passion) certainly overpowers him, as does the wind a weak tree.

8. Asubhānupassiṁ viharantaṁ
indriyesu susaṁvutaṁ
bhojanamhi ca mattaññuṁ
saddhaṁ āraddhavīriyaṁ,
taṁ ve nappasahati Māro
vāto selaṁ'va pabbataṁ.

He who lives seeing the filthiness (of the body), whose senses are well controlled, who is moderate in food, is devoted and energetic, *Māra* certainly does not overpower him, as the wind a rocky mountain.

Explanation 7-8

The mind is defiled by internal enemies like passions,

greed, hatred etc. which stand in the way of enlightenment. One who is under the sway of these evil propensities cannot tread on the path of spiritual achievements being a victim of internal enemies. Those who are morally strong, patient, zealous and have firm faith in their missions defeat the internal enemies to reach the zenith of brilliant achievements.

9. Anikkasāvo kāsāvaṁ
yo vatthaṁ paridahessati
apeto damasaccena,
na so kāsāvaṁ arahati.

Whosoever shall put on the yellow robe, himself not being free from impurity and being devoid of self-control and truth, he does not really deserve the yellow robe.

10. Yo ca vantakāsāv'assa
silesu susamāhito
upeto damasaccena,
sa ve kāsāvaṁ arahati.

One who has purged oneself of impurities, is well-established in morals, is endowed with self-control and truth, he indeed is worthy of the yellow robe.

11. Asāre sāramatino
sāre cāsāradassino,
te sāraṁ nādhigacchanti
micchāsaṅak ppagocarā.

Those who take the non-essential to be essential and the essential to be non-essential, they do not attain the essential, living in the sphere of wrong aims.

12. Sārañ ca sārato ñatvā
asārañ ca asārato,
te sāraṁ adhigacchanti
sammāsaṅkappagocarā.

Those who know the essential as essential and the non-essential as the non-essential, do attain the essential, being in the sphere of right aims.

Explanation 11-12

The life which is ceaselessly troubled and tormented by worldly matters and engirdled by the cycle of birth and death is not a meaningless jargon. There lies hidden the supreme reality. As it does not reveal itself to the superficial view, the momentary happiness and miseries of life and the day-to-day affairs loom large and appear as reality. Such dull-headed persons can never attain the reality leaving aside the dull dredgry surface of life and waste away their days in delusion like the deer running after mirage in the desert.

When the veil of ignorance goes off from the inner eyes of those who go deeper and deeper in search of truth, they view the world in its true perspective. The light of the Supreme truth dawns on them.

13. Yathā agāraṁ ducchannaṁ
vuṭṭhi samativijjhati,
evaṁ abi āvitaṁ cittaṁ
rāgo samativijjhati.

As rain penetrates an ill-thatched house, so lust penetrates an undeveloped mind.

14. Yathā agāraṁ succhannaṁ
vuṭṭhi na samativijjhati,
evaṁ subhāvitaṁ cittaṁ
rāgo na samativijjhati.

As rain does not penetrate a well-thatched house, so lust does not penetrate a well-developed mind.

Explanation 13-14

Our natural mind is pure and transparent, which gets defiled, debased and degenerated because of the bad or immoral mental faculties like lust, hatred etc. If the mind is kept free from these defilements, it develops like a flower-bud in fragrance and beauty and remains immersed in bliss. The cultivation of mental exercise is necessary to rid the mind of the clutches of evil propensities. Lust etc. cannot find access into such a well meditative mind.

15. Idha socati, pecca socati,
pāpakāī ubhayattha socati;
so socati, so vihaññati,
disvā kammakiliṭṭhamattano.

Here he grieves; hereafter he grieves; the sinful man grieves in both the places; seeing his impure actions he grieves and perishes.

16. Idha modati, pecca modati,
katapuñño ubhayattha modati;
so modati, so pamodati,
disvā kammavisuddhimattano.

Here he rejoices; hereafter he rejoices; the virtuous man rejoices in both the places; seeing his pure actions he rejoices and rejoices exceedingly.

17. Idha tappati, pecca tappati,
pāpakārī ubhayattha tappati;
pāpaṁ me katan ti tappati,
bhiyyo tappati duggatiṁ gato.

Here he laments, hereafter he laments, the sinful man laments in both the places; 'I committed sin', thus he laments; he laments all the more having gone to an evil existence.

18. Idha nandati, pecca nandati,
katapuñño ubhayattha nandati;
puññaṁ me katan ti nandati,
bhiyyo nandati suggatiṁ gato.

Here he delights; hereafter he delights; the virtuous man delights in both the places; 'I have done good', thus he delights; he delights all the more having gone to a blissful existence.

19. Bahum pi ce sahitaṁ bhāsamāno
na takkaro hoti naro pamatto
gopo'va gāvo gaṇayaṁ paresaṁ
na bhāgavā sāmaññassa hoti.

Though a person recites much of the Sacred Texts, yet, if he, being negligent, does not live up to them, he will not share the holy life like the cowherd who counts the kine of others.

20. Appam pi ce sahitaṁ bhāsamāno
dhammassa hoti anudhammacārī
rāgañ ca dosañ ca pahāya mohaṁ
sammappajāno suvimuttacitto
anupādiyāno idha vā huraṁ vā,
sa bhāgavā sāmaññassa hoti.

Though a person recites but a little of the Sacred Texts, yet, if he lives up to the Teaching, having dispelled, his lust, hatred and deception, possessing right knowledge with a mind well-freed and not clinging to this world or the next, he does indeed share the holy life.

Explanation 19-20

As one cannot have the taste of sweets by merely carrying the same on his head, so one who recites much from the sacred texts without following the teachings, cannot have the blessings of supreme attainments prescribed for. One may, however, recite little from the texts, but follows the teachings in letter and spirit and dives into the depths of *Dhamma*, such a one having freed himself from all fetters is really blessed with the bliss of supreme attainments.

Yamakavaggo Pathamo

2. APPAMĀDAVAGGA
(AWAKENING)

1. Appamādo amatapadaṁ,
pamādo maccuno padaṁ,
appamattā na mīyanti,
ye pamattā yathāmatā.

Vigilance is the path to Immortality (*Nibbāna*); negligence is the path to death; vigilant people do not die, those who are negligent are like unto the dead.

2. Etaṁ visesato ñatvā
appamādamhi paṇḍitā,
appamāde pamodanti
ariyānaṁ gocare ratā.

The wise distinctly realising this (difference) in vigilance, rejoice in it devoted to the life of the Noble ones (*Āryas*).

3. Te jhāyino sātatikā
niccaṁ daḷhaparakkamā,
phusanti dhīrā nibbāṇaṁ
yogakkhemaṁ anuttaraṁ.

Those wise men who are always absorbed in meditation, ever exerting their best, realise *Nibbāna* (the Summum Bonum) the incomparable state of security.

Explanation 1-3

When one is in the grip of delusion, one's vision is blurred and cannot see things in their true perspective. Such a person imagines the world as the repository of pleasures. In his superficial view the sensual enjoyment is the summum bonum of life. His intense desire for enjoyment goads him to plunge himself into it. In other words, he discards good ways of life and follows the wrong path. Such reckless living is sleepiness which prevents him from marching ahead towards the ultimate goal—the realisation of *Nibbāna.* In one word sleepiness stands in the way to spiritual progress. The absence of progress spells ruin or death. Hence sleepiness is considered as the way to death and the sleepy persons are as good as dead.

Awakening means the dawn of wisdom by getting rid of sleepiness. In a congenial atmosphere due to noble company and admonition etc. when one awakes, the worldly pleasures hold no charms for him and the world appears empty like the bubbles or mirage. His mind gets fed up with the world and seeks solace within. He aspires after marching forward towards the supreme goal leaving behind everything else. In fact, this is the beginning of a noble march. Hence awakening is regarded as the way to immortality.

4. Uṭṭhānavato satimato
sucikammassa nisammakārino
saññatassa ca dhammajīvino
appamattassayaso'bhivaḍḍhati.

His glory increases more and more who is energetic, mindful, blameless in deed, discriminative, self-restrained, righteous and vigilant.

5. Uṭṭhānen'appamādena
saññamena damena ca
dīpaṁ kayirātha medhāvi
yaṁ ogho nābhikīrati.

Let the wise person, by energy, vigilance, discipline and self-control, make an island for himself that may not be overwhelmed by flood.

Explanation 5

The mind of being is often flooded by base passions. Surrounded by various sufferings he is tossed in the endless ocean of rebirths. He finds himself helpless there. In order to get rid of the helpless miserable state one should exert to build such a refuge for oneself as cannot be endangered by anything.

6. Pamādamanuyuñjanti
bālā dummedhino janā,
appamādañ ca medhāvī
dhanaṁ seṭṭhaṁ va rakkhati.

The ignorant, foolish people indulge in negligence, the wise person guards vigilance as a valuable wealth.

7. Mā pamādamanuyuñjetha,
mā kāmaratisanthavaṁ;
appamatto hi jhāyanto
pappoti vipulaṁ sukham.

Do not indulge in negligence; have no intimacy with sensual pleasures. The vigilant person engaged in meditation attains great happiness.

Explanation 6-7

The unwise and the thoughtless people plunge themselves into worldly pleasures in the absence of knowledge about the consequences. But the wise are aware of the benefits of awakening. Hence they are constantly alert that ignorance and delusion may not grip their minds to distress. Thus they maintain the state of awakening very dearly. Those who keep awake and meditate are blessed with bliss and peace within. Hence the Buddha exhorts: Indulge not in sleepiness, nor in sensual pleasures, but cultivate meditation.

8. Pamādaṁ appamādena
yadā nudati paṇḍito,
paññāpāsādamāruyha
asoko sokiniṁ pajam,
pabbataṭṭho'va bhummaṭṭhe,
dhīro bāle avekkhati.

When the wise person expels negligence by vigilance, then he, having ascended the palace of wisdom, himself being free from sorrow, beholds the sorrowing ignorant mankind, as one that is on the top of a mountain beholds those who are below.

Explanation 8

The descent of brilliant light of super knowledge glorifies the inmost being of one who drives away the darkness of delusion and ignorance by awakening. At this stage he remains unaffected by all happenings around and soars high above the unwise suffering masses.

9. Appamatto pamattesu
suttesu bahujāgaro
abalassaṁ'va sīghasso
hitvā yāti sumedhaso.

The wise man that is vigilant among the negligent, and wakeful among the sleeping, surpasses all, as a strong horse outdistances a weak one.

Explanation 9

The sleepy and slothful people find an access to the world of bliss and peace in the absence of awakening. Their upward march is a myth. Therefore, they are left behind by the wakeful wise one who marches ahead towards the goal of *Nibbāna* transgressing the mundane limits.

10. Appamādena Maghavā
devānaṁ seṭṭhataṁ gato;
appamādaṁ pasaṁsanti
pamādo garahito sadā.

By vigilance Maghavā (the King of gods) became chief of the gods; vigilance is praised and negligence is ever despised.

11. Appamādarato bhikkhu
pamāde bhayadassi vā
saññojanaṁ anuṁ thūlaṁ
ḍahaṁ aggī va gacchati.

The monk who is devoted to vigilance and views negligence with fear, advances on like a fire burning the fetters, great and small.

12. Appamādarato bhikkhu
pamāde bhayadassi vā
abhabbo parihāṇāya,
nibbāṇass'eva santike.

The monk who is devoted to vigilance and views negligence with fear, is not liable to fall, he is close to *Nibbāna.*

Appamādavaggo Dutiyo

Explanation 11-12

One who awakes from sleepiness, would not like to relapse into sleepiness darkened by delusion and ignorance. He dreads sleepiness and gets alert so that it may not revert to play havoc with his awakening. Such a person getting awakened, goes ahead with the cultivation of meditation burning and melting all fetters in the fire of spiritual culture. He never deviates from the path and reaches the supreme goal in due course.

3. CHITTAVAGGA
(THE MIND)

1. Phandanaṁ capalaṁ cittaṁ
durakkhaṁ dunnivārayaṁ
ujuṁ karoti medhāvī
usukāro'va tejanaṁ.

The wise man straightens the mind that is trembling, fickle and difficult to guard and control, as a fletcher straightens an arrow.

Explanation 1

The mind wavers constantly like ripples in a river and is never still and steady. It wanders aimlessly from one object to the other without being fixed on a particular object. It is very difficult to bring it under control or prevent it from going astray. However, the wise one tames and trains such mind for greater purpose through spiritual culture.

2. Vārijo'va thale khitto
okamokata ubbhato,
pariphandati'daṁ cittaṁ
Māradheyyaṁ pahātave.

As a fish taken out of its watery abode and cast on the land, so struggles this mind to escape from the realm of *Māra* (the Evil One).

Explanation 2

Naturally the mind is desirous of peace and happiness. The crazy thirst for the same makes it restless. Since the actual source of peace and happiness is not within its knowledge it roams at random in search of the same, but to no purpose. As the child wanting its mother feels uneasy with others, so the mind desirous of peace and happiness finds no satisfaction in transient matters of the world and struggles to transgress the mundane limit for eternal peace and bliss of *Nibbāna.*

3. Dunniggahassa lahuno
   yatthakāmanipātino
   cittassa damatho sādhu;
   cittaṁ dantaṁ sukhāvahaṁ.

It is good to control the mind which is hard to control and which is flighty and flits wherever it likes; the mind brought under control brings happiness.

4. Sududdasaṁ sunipuṇaṁ
   yatthakāmanipātinaṁ
   cittaṁ rakkhetha medhāvī;
   cittaṁ guttaṁ sukhāvahaṁ.

Let the wise person guard the mind, which is difficult to perceive, extremely subtle and which flits wherever it likes, the guarded mind brings happiness.

Explanation 3-4

Mind is naturally perverse, chooses a wrong path and indulges in wrong matters. Those who do or behave as desired by mind instead of controlling it, are prone to going astray and bring ruin to themselves consequently. Those who restrain the mind and follow the right path march towards the supreme goal of *Nibbāna* and put an end to all sufferings. Hence, the control of mind is the fountain of felicity.

5. Dūraṅgamaṁ ekacaraṁ
asarīraṁ guhāsayaṁ
ye cittaṁ saññamessanti,
mokkhanti Mārabandhanā.

Those who control the mind that travels far, wanders alone, is without a body and lies in the cave (of heart), escape from the fetter of *Māra.*

Explanation 5

The control of mind is a must to become free from all fetters like lust, hatred, etc. with a view to reaching the supreme goal of *Nibbāna.*

6. Anavaṭṭhitacittassa
saddhammaṁ avijānato
pariplavapasādassa
paññā na paripūrati.

His wisdom will never be perfect whose mind is not steadfast, who does not know the True Doctrine and whose faith is wavering.

7. Anavassutacittassa
ananvāhatacetaso
puññapāpapahīnassa
natthi jāgarato bhayaṁ.

There is no fear for such a watchful one whose mind is not saturated by lust, nor affected by hatred and who has abandoned good and evil.

8. Kumbhūpamaṁ kāyaṁ imaṁ viditvā,
nagarūpamaṁ cittaṁ idaṁ ṭhapetvā,
yodhetha Māraṁ paññāyudhena,
jitañ ca rakkhe, anivesano siyā.

Knowing this body to be (fragile) as a clay pot, establishing this mind as (firm as) a (well fortified) city, let one attack *Māra* with the weapon of wisdom and guard one's conquest and be without attachment.

Explanation 8

A common man's attachment to his own body knows no bounds. He leaves no stone unturned to provide ease and comfort to the body. He can throw to the wind all canons of conduct and good virtues for the sake of it. Thus, the intense attachment darkens his life. This transient body will have to be cast away like the used earthen pot at the end. Bearing in mind the transitory nature of the body one should eschew the deep attachment for it, guard one's mind like a fortified city and fight the internal enemies like lust, hatred, etc. At the same time one should be alert that one's upward march is not hampered. This is the admonition of the Buddha.

9. Aciraṁ vat'ayaṁ kāyo
pa̤thaviṁ adhisessati
chuddho apetaviññāṇo
niratthaṁ'va kaliṅgaraṁ.

Before long alas! this body will lie on the earth, cast aside, devoid of consciousness, as a useless log.

10. Diso disaṁ yaṁ taṁ kayirā
verī vā pana verinaṁ,
micchāpaṇihitaṁ cittaṁ
pāpiyo naṁ tato kare.

Whatever (harm) a hater may do to one he hates or an enemy to his enemy, an ill-directed mind may do one greater harm than that.

11. Na taṁ mātā pitā kayirā
aññe vāpi ca ñātakā,
sammāpaṇihitaṁ cittaṁ
seyyaso naṁ tato kare.

Neither mother nor father nor any other relative may do a person greater good than his well-directed mind may do him.

Explanation 11

The progress and regress of life depend on the good and bad tendencies of mind respectively. According to its tendency one's life gets dirty and distressful, while the other's becomes bright and blissful.

By misdirecting the mind one does more harm to oneself, because it brings forth disastrous results. One who puts the mind on the right track makes the life bright and blissful and march towards the supreme goal.

Cittavaggo Tatiyo

4. PUPPHAVAGGA
(FLOWERS)

1. Ko imaṁ paṭhaviṁ vijessati
   Yamalokañ ca imaṁ sadevakaṁ?
   ko dhammapadaṁ sudesitaṁ
   kusalo puppham iva pacessati?

Who shall conquer this earth, the realm of *Yama* (the ruler of the kingdom of the dead) and this world of gods? Who shall gather the well-preached Teachings as a clever (garland-maker) gathers flowers?

2. Sekho paṭhaviṁ vijessati?
   Yamalokañ ca imaṁ sadevakaṁ,
   sekho dhammapadaṁ sudesitam
   kusalo puppham iva pacessati.

The Sekha (those who have attained one of the seven stages, from Sotapatti Magga to Arhantta Magga) shall conquer this earth, the realm of *Yama* and this world of gods; he alone shall gather the Teachings as a clever (garland-maker) gathers flowers.

Explanation 1-2

Since a disciple who is morally trained, mentally developed and enlightened within, realises the impermanent and sorrowful world in its true perspective, he conquers all cravings for the world. Thus he reflects the well-preached maxims of *Dhamma* in his own life.

3. Pheṇūpamaṁ kāyam imaṁ viditvā
marīcidhammaṁ abhisambudhāno
chetvāna Mārassa papupphakāni
adassanaṁ Maccusājassa gacche.

Knowing this body to be as a foam and understanding its mirage-like nature, one should escape the sight of the King of Death, having destroyed the flower shafts of *Māra.*

Explanation 3

As the attachment to body blinds one's vision one cannot comprehend the true nature of the body, consequently one's egotism grows by leaps and bounds retarding the upward march. So one is far away from the path of immortality. The Buddha admonishes that realising the nature of body which is frail and full of impure substances, one should eschew egotism, root out lust, hatred etc. and leave the cycle of birth and death.

4. Pupphāni h'eva pacinantaṁ
byāsattamanasaṁ naraṁ
suttaṁ gāmaṁ mahogho'va
maccu ādāya gacchati.

While a man gathers flowers (of sense-pleasures) and his mind is attached to them, death carries him off, as a sleeping village is carried off by a great flood.

5. Pupphāni h'eva pacinantaṁ
byāsattamanasaṁ naraṁ
atittaṁ yeva kāmesu
antako kurute vasaṁ.

While a man gathers flowers (of sense-pleasures) and his mind is attached to them, he is overpowered by death before he satisfies himself with them.

Explanation 5

As a gardener goes on plucking flowers assiduously in the garden, so a common man pursues worldly matters eagerly. His mind is in the grip of wild desires. Thus his days glide away unnoticed. Alas! the chilled hand of death snatches him away unawares.

6. Yathā pi bhamaro pupphaṁ
vaṇṇagandhaṁ aheṭhayaṁ
paleti rasam ādāya,
evaṁ gāme munī care.

As the bee flies away, having collected honey without injuring the beauty and the scent of the flowers, so let the Sage wander in the village (for alms).

7. Na paresaṁ vilomāni,
na paresaṁ katākataṁ
attano va avekkheyya
katāni akatāni ca.

Let one not look into the faults of others and their actions done and left undone; let one look into one's actions done and left undone.

Explanation 7

One wounds one's own feelings only by finding faults with others. It is no use disturbing one's own mind thereby. Instead of looking into what has been done or not done by others one should probe one's own doings. This serves to improve one's character.

8. Yathāpi ruciraṁ pupphaṁ
vaṇṇavantaṁ agandhakaṁ,
evaṁ subhāsitā vācā
aphalā hoti akubbato.

As a beautiful flower full of colour but devoid of scent, so the good words of a man, who does not act according to them, are useless.

9. Yathāpi ruciraṁ pupphaṁ
vaṇṇavantaṁ sagandhakaṁ,
evaṁ subhāsitā vācā
saphalā hoti sakubbato.

As a beautiful flower full of colour and scent, so the good words of a man who acts according to them, are useful.

10. Yathāpi puppharāsimhā,
kayirā mālāguṇe bahū
evaṁ jātena maccena
kattabbaṁ kusalaṁ bahuṁ.

As many kinds of garlands may be made from heap of flowers, so much good should be done by one born a mortal.

Explanation 10

Human birth is itself a blessing, since a man possesses the right of uplifting himself. One should not let slip this advantage by wasting away one's days, but make an endeavour for one's uplift by doing good deeds.

11. Na pupphagandho paṭivātam eti,
na candanaṁ tagaramallikā vā,
satañ ca gandho paṭivātam eti,
sabbā disā sappuriso pavāti.

The scent of flowers does not blow against the wind nor of sandalwood, tagara and of jasmine. But the fragrance of the virtuous does blow against the wind and the man of virtue pervades all directions.

12. Candanaṁ tagaraṁ vāpi
uppalaṁ atha vassikī,
etesaṁ gandhajātānaṁ
sīlagandho anuttaro.

Of all perfumes such as sandalwood, tagara, lotus and jasmine, the perfume of virtue is by far the best.

13. Appamatto ayaṁ gandho
yāyaṁ tagaracandanī,
yo ca sīlavataṁ gandho
vāti devesu uttamo.

This fragrance of tagara and sandalwood is of little account. The excellent fragrance of the virtuous blows among the gods.

14. Tesaṁ sampannasīlānaṁ
appamādavihārinaṃ
sammadaññāvimuttānaṁ
Māro maggaṁ na vindati.

Māra does not find the path of those who are full of virtue, vigilant in living and are fully emancipated through perfect knowledge.

Explanation 14

The best of all perfumes is that of virtue of the virtuous. The perfume of the various fragrant things stands no comparison with that of virtue. No evil befalls those who are virtuous, enlightened and free from fetters.

15. Yathā saṅkāradhānasmiṁ
ujjhitasmiṁ mahāpathe

padumaṁ tattha jāyetha
sucigandhaṁ manoramaṁ.

As a sweet scented attractive lotus may grow on a heap of rubbish thrown at the highway.

16. Evaṁ saṅkārabhūtesu
andhabhūte puthujjane
atirocati paññāya
Sammāsambuddhasāvako.

Even so, the disciple of the fully Enlightened One outshines in wisdom amongst the ignorant worldlings who are like rubbish.

Explanation 16

As the blossomed lotus grown in the muddy marsh displays its splendour of beauty and fragrance, so a holy seer of truth soars high above the common mass of men and shines in glory of bright virtues and wisdom.

Pupphavaggo Catuttho

5. BĀLAVAGGA
(FOOLS)

1. Dīghā jāgarato ratti,
dīghaṁ santassa yojanaṁ,
dīgho bālānaṁ saṁsāro
saddhammaṁ avijānataṁ.

The night is long to the wakeful, the league is long to the person who is tired, the round of birth and death too long to the ignorant who do not know the sublime Doctrine.

Explanation 1

The night appears to be long to the sleepless and the path shows no end to the weary. Likewise, the worldly pleasures appear to be endless to those who neither keep company with the wise, nor hear the noble sayings. Immersed in the depth of ignorance they find no way to immortality. Consequently, their world-wandering lengthens.

2. Carañ ce nādhigaccheyya
seyyaṁ sadisam attano,
ekacariyaṁ daḷhaṁ kayirā,
natthi bāle sahāyatā.

If a seeker does not find a friend better than or equal

to him, let him resolutely pursue a solitary life; for there is no fellowship with a fool.

Explanation 2

The company that a man keeps, serves as a base for character-building. There is an adage that good company is the source of happiness, while bad company ruins one. One should, therefore, be cautious to select companions. First of all, one may seek company of the better persons. If not available, one should find companions of equal virtues. In the absence of them one should live alone doing one's own duties.

3. 'Puttā m'atthi dhana m'atthi'
iti bālo vihaññati,
attā hi attano natthi
kuto puttā kuto dhanaṁ?

'There are my sons, there is my wealth', thus worries the fool. He himself is not his own. What to speak of sons and wealth?

Explanation 3

A fool favoured with fortune and sons gets puffed up and madly pursues pleasures leaving the path of virtue. Such a person brings ruin to himself only through his own folly. In the world evidently even he himself is not his own, not to speak of wealth and sons. Death dissolves one's body and mind in no time.

4. Yo bālo maññati bālyaṁ,
pаṇḍito vāpi tena so,
bālo ca paṇḍitamānī
sa ve bālo 'ti vuccati.

A fool who knows his folly is a wise man on that account. The fool who thinks that he is wise is a veritable fool.

Explanation 4

A fool who is aware of his foolishness can no longer remain a fool, but makes an effort to develop his understanding. Thus, he becomes gradually wise. But a fool who considers himself wise, indulges in his foolishness only. Wisdom never dawns on him.

5. Yāvajivam 'pi ce bālo
paṇḍitaṁ payirupāsati,
na so dhammaṁ vijānāti
dabbi sūparasaṁ yathā.

Though a fool associates with a wise man for the whole of his life yet he fails to realise the Law, as a ladle the taste of the soup.

Explanation 5

Due to ignorance the foolish folk indulge in sinful deeds. Thereby they bring about their own ruin and spoil their own future. Thus they become their own enemies.

6. Muhuttam api ce viññū
paṇḍitaṁ payirupāsati,
khippaṁ dhammaṁ vijānāti
jivhā sūparasaṁ yathā.

If an intelligent man associates with a wise man even for a moment immediately he realises the Law, as the tongue the flavour of the soup.

7. Caranti bālā dummedhā
amitten'eva attanā
karontā pāpakaṁ kammaṁ,
yaṁ hoti kaṭukapphalaṁ.

As a deep pool, extremely clear and unperturbed, so the wise become extremely pure by listening to the Doctrine.

Explanation 7

Like pouring of water into a leaky jar meaningless is the hearing of *Dhamma* for those who lack understanding. But as soon as the wise hear the *Dhamma*, their awakened minds go deep into it and become calm and blissful.

8. No taṁ kammaṁ kataṁ sādhu
yaṁ katvā anutappati,
yassa assumukho rodaṁ
vipākaṁ paṭisevati.

The righteous indeed renounce (attachment for) everything. Sages do not talk for their own ends. Touched either by happiness or misery, the wise are not elated or depressed.

Explanation 8

The saintly persons who seek after truth, give up longings for worldly matters and their conversations smack of no cravings. Being absorbed in noble thoughts they remain unaffected by happiness and misery.

9. Tañ ca kammaṁ kataṁ sādhu
yaṁ katvā nānutappati,
yassa patīto sumano
vipākaṁ paṭisevati.

One should not wish for a son, wealth or a kingdom for one's own sake or for the sake of others; one should not wish one's own prosperity by unfair means. Such a one is virtuous, wise and righteous.

10. Madhu'vā maññatī bālo
yāva pāpaṁ na paccati,
yadā ca paccati pāpaṁ
atha bālo dukkhaṁ nigacchati.

There are only a few among men who go across. The rest of the people return to this very shore.

11. Māse māse kusaggena
bālo bhuñjetha bhojanaṁ,
na so saṅkhatadhammānaṁ
kalaṁ agghati soḷasiṁ.

Those who act according to well-expounded Truth, will reach the other shore, crossing the realm of death so difficult to cross.

Explanation 11

Those whose vision is directed towards *Nibbāna* piercing the veil of ignorance and delusion and who strive hard to reach the Supreme goal are a microscopic minority. All others infatuated with passion for earthly pleasures waste away the days of life. Those who inspired with the ideals of the noble ones follow the path expounded by them, go beyond the cycle of birth and death and put an end to sufferings.

12. Na hi pāpaṁ kataṁ kammaṁ,
sajju khīraṁ'va muccati,
ḍahantaṁ bālam anveti,
bhasmacchanno'va pāvako.

The wise man should cultivate the good having discarded the evil. Going from home to the homelessness, to the solitude, which is difficult to enjoy.

13. Yāvadeva anatthāya
ñattaṁ bālassa jāyati,
hanti bālassa sukkaṁsaṁ
muddham assa vipātayaṁ.

So far the knowledge of a fool leads to his own calamity, it cleaves his head and destroys his better lot.

14. Asataṁ bhāvanam iccheyya,
purekkhārañ ca bhikkhusu,
āvāsesu ca issariyaṁ,
pujā parakulesu ca.

The foolish monk will wish for undeserving reputation, precedence amongst monks, authority in monasteries, honour among the families.

15. "Mam'eva kata maññantu,
gihī pabbajitā ubho,
mam'evativasā assu
kiccākiccesu kismici"
iti bālassa saṅkappo
icchā māno ca vaḍḍhati.

'Let the laymen and the monks both think that this was done by me; let them be under me in every work great or small'; thus wishes the fool and his desires and egotism increase.

16. Aññā hi lābhūpanisā,
aññā nibbānagāminī,
evam etaṁ abhiññāya,
bhikkhu Buddhassa sāvako
sakkāraṁ nābhinandeyya,
vivekam anubrūhaye.

Indeed the path that leads to worldly gains is one and the path that leads to *Nibbāna* is quite another. Thus the monk who is a disciple of the Buddha knowing this, should not delight in worldly favours, but should develop loneliness.

Explanation 16

Nibbāna is the goal of Bhikkhuhood, but not wealth and fame. The way to *Nibbāna* is different therefrom. One who wants to drink deep in the fountain of peace and bliss of *Nibbāna*, should engage oneself vigorously in the pursuit of spiritual development for the attainment of *Nibbāna* leaving behind worldly gains.

Bālavaggo Pañcamo

6. PAṆḌITAVAGGA
(WISE)

1. Nidhīnaṁ'va pavattāraṁ
yaṁ passe vajjadassinaṁ,
niggayhavādiṁ medhāviṁ
tādisaṁ paṇḍitaṁ bhaje,
tādisaṁ bhajamānassa
seyyo hoti na pāpiyo.

Should one see a wise man who points out faults and reproves them, one should associate with such a wise man, considering him as one who points out a hidden treasure; it will be for the better and not for the worse, to one who keeps company with such a man.

2. Ovadeyyānusāseyya,
asabbhā ca nivāraye,
sataṁ hi so piyo hoti,
asataṁ hoti appiyo.

One should admonish, instruct and prevent others from evils; for, such a one is dear to the righteous, but unpleasant to the wicked.

3. Na bhaje pāpake mitte,
na bhaje purisādhame,
bhajetha mitte kalyāṇe,
bhajetha purisuttame.

Do not associate with evil friends; and do not associate with those who are mean. Associate only with righteous friends; and associate with those who are noble.

4. Dhammapīti sukhaṁ seti
vippasannena cetasa,
ariyappavedite dhamme
sadā ramati paṇḍito.

One who delights in the Truth dwells happily with a serene mind. The wise man always delights in the Law preached by the Noble One.

5. Udakaṁ hi nayanti nettikā,
usukārā namayanti tejanaṁ,
dāruṁ namayanti tacchakā,
attānaṁ damayanti paṇḍitā.

Irrigators lead the water; fletchers fashion the arrow; carpenters bend the wood; the wise control themselves.

Explanation 5

As carpenters shape the wood into various forms, arrow-makers make the arrow-shafts straight and irrigators direct the course of water as desired, so the wise achieve greatness through self-control.

6. Selo yathā ekaghano
vātena na samīrati,

evaṁ nindāpasaṁsāsu
na samiñjanti paṇḍitā.

As a solid rock is not shaken by the wind, so the wise are not moved by blame or praise.

7. Yathāpi rahado gambhīro
vippasanno anāvilo,
evaṁ dhammāni sutvāna
vippasīdantī paṇḍitā.

The fools of little understanding with the very self as their own foe, wander about doing sinful actions, the result of which is bitter.

8. Subbattha ve sappurisā cajanti
na kāmakāmā lapayanti santo,
sukhena phuṭṭhā athavā dukhena
na uccāvacaṁ paṇḍitā dassayanti.

That action is not well done which having done, one repents and the result of which one reaps weeping with tearful face.

9. Na attahetu, na parassa hetu,
na puttamicche na dhanaṁ na raṭṭhaṁ,
na iccheyya adhammena samiddhim attano,
sa sīlavā paññavā dhammiko siyā.

That action is well done, which having done, one does not repent and the result of which one reaps gladly and cheerfully.

Explanation 8-9

Karma is the guiding force behind one's happiness and unhappiness. A good deed brings forth good results and a bad deed bad results. One should, therefore, refrain from deeds yielding bad results and do such deeds as would make one's life happy and blissful.

10. Appakā te manussesu
ye janā pāragāmino,
athāyaṁ itarā pajā
tīramevānudhāvati.

The fool considers a sinful action as sweet as honey so long as it ripens not. When the sinful action ripens then the fool comes to grief.

11. Ye ca kho sammadakkhāte
dhamme dhammānuvattino,
te janā pāramessanti
maccudheyyaṁ suduttaraṁ.

A fool may eat as much as he can catch with the end of a grass-blade at the expiry of each month. Yet he is not worth even the sixteenth part of them who have realised the Noble Law.

Explanation 11

A fool may take as little food as possible by way of practising austerities, but he is far away from the truth. Such a person stands no comparison to those who have realised the truth.

12. Kaṇhaṁ dhammaṁ vippahāya
sukkaṁ bhāvetha paṇḍito,
okā anokaṁ āgamma
viveke yattha dūramaṁ.

The sinful action does not bear fruit immediately as the milk that does not turn into curd at once. Smouldering it follows the fool like a fire covered with ashes.

13. Tatrābhiratim iccheyya
hitvā kāme akiñcano,
pariyodapeyya attānaṁ
cittaklesehi paṇḍito.

There he should delight, giving up sensual pleasures, possessing nothing, the wise man should purify himself of all mental defilements.

Explanation 12-13

One whose inner eye is opened, is disposed to live a life of purity dispelling the dark qualities. Leaving the defiled atmosphere of the worldlings such a one becomes a homeless recluse and cleanses oneself of the impurities of mind through cultivation of moral and spiritual virtues to march ahead towards the supreme goal of *Nibbāna*.

14. Yesaṁ sambodhiaṅgesu
sammā cittam subhāvitaṁ,
ādānapaṭinissagge
anupādāya ye ratā,
Khīṇāsavā jutīmanto,
te loke parinibbutā.

Those whose mind is well developed in the Factors of Enlightenment, who, not clinging to anything, delight in the renunciation of attachment, are free from corruption and shine, they have attained *Nibbāna* in this world.

Paṇḍitavaggo Chaṭṭhamo

7. ARAHANTAVAGGA
(THE SINLESS)

1. Gataddhino visokassa
vippamuttassa sabbadhi
sabbaganthappahīnassa
pariḷāho na vijjati.

There is no anguish for him who has ended his journey and is freed from all grief, is emancipated in every way and has destroyed all ties.

2. Uyyuñjanti satīmanto,
na nikete ramanti te,
haṁsā'va pallalaṁ hitvā
okam okaṁ jahanti te.

They being mindful ever exert themselves and never delight in a home. As the swans that quit a pool, they abandon all homes.

Explanation 2

The mindful awakened sages always exert themselves for their spiritual wealth and uplift. They remain unattached by abandoning all worldly defilements. As ducks quit the pools with detachment after finishing the search for food, so the fetterless sages do not feel embarrassed with the thoughts of 'I' and mine.

3. Yesaṁ sannicayo natthi,
ye pariññātabhojanā,
suññato animitto ca
vimokkho yesaṁ gocaro,
ākāse'va sakuntānaṁ
gati tesaṁ durannayā.

Those who do not accumulate and reflect well over their food, and whose object is deliverance, the void, the signless, their path cannot be traced like that of birds in the air.

4. Yassāsavā parikkhīṇā
āhāre ca anissito,
suññato animitto ca
vimokkho yassa gocaro,
ākāse'va sakuntānaṁ
padaṁ tassa durannayaṁ.

Whose defilements have come to an end, who is not attached to food and whose object is deliverance, the void, the signless, their path cannot be traced like that of birds in the air.

Explanation 3-4

Unknown is the supreme goal of those who worry not for future, take their meals for the maintenance of the physical frame without any attachment and drink deep in the fountain of bliss of *Nibbāna* having the causeless Deliverance devoid of lust, hatred etc.

5. Yass'indriyāni samathaṁgatāni,
assā yathā sārathinā sudantā,
pahīṇamānassa anāsavassa
devāpi tassa pihayanti tādino.

Even the gods hold with esteem such a one whose senses have been calmed, like the horses brought under control by the charioteer and who has dispelled his conceit and is free from corruption.

6. Paṭhavīsamo no virujjhati,
indakhīlūpamo tādi subbato,
rahado'va apetakaddamo,
saṁsārā na bhavanti tādino.

There are no more life's wanderings for such a one who resents not like the earth, as firm in character as a gate post, as pure as a deep pool free from mud.

Explanation 5-6

Such a pious one remains unperturbed like the earth, steadfast like pillar and is lustrous like a lake unsullied by mud. His sojourn of life or rebirth comes to an end.

7. Santaṁ tassa manaṁ hoti
santā vācā ca kamma ca,
sammadaññāvimuttassa
upasantassa tādino.

His mind is calm, his word is calm and his deed is calm, who, rightly knowing, is wholly freed and perfectly peaceful.

Explanation 7

Calm and peaceful are the mind, speech and deed of a sage who has freed himself from all fetters by traversing the path of enlightenment and merged himself in the depth of peace by extinguishing the fire of lust, hatred etc.

8. Assaddho akataññū ca
sandhicchedo ca yo naro,
hatāvakāso vantāso
sa ve uttamaporiso.

He indeed is a noble person who is not credulous, understands the Uncreate (*Nibbāna*), has cut off the fetters (of birth and death), has put an end to existence and has renounced every desire.

9. Gāme vā yadi vā raññe,
ninne vā yadī vā thale,
yatthārahanto viharanti
taṁ bhūmiṁ rāmaṇeyyakaṁ.

Whether in village or in forest, whether in low-land or in high-land, wherever the worthy (*Arahants*) dwell that spot is delightful.

10. Ramaṇiyāni araññāni,
yattha na ramatī jano,
vītarāgā ramissanti,
na te kāmagavesino.

Charming are the forests where no worldlings find delight; those who have destroyed passions do delight there, for, they are not after sensual pleasures.

Arahantavaggo Sattamo

8. SAHASSAVAGGA
(THE THOUSANDS)

1. Sahassam api ce vācā
anatthapadasaṁhitā,
ekaṁ atthapadaṁ seyyo
yaṁ sutvā upasammati.

A single word full of meaning, hearing which one is at peace, is better than thousand useless words.

2. Sahassam api ce gāthā
anatthapadasaṁhitā,
ekaṁ gāthāpadaṁ seyyo
yaṁ sutvā upasammati.

A single verse, hearing which one is at peace, is better than thousand useless verses.

Explanation 1-2

The uttering of one sentence or stanza that opens the eye of wisdom, pacifies the burning within and brings the bliss of *Nibbāna* is far better than uttering a thousand sentences or stanzas of no meaning.

3. Yo ca gathāsataṁ bhāse
anatthapadasaṁhitā,

ekaṁ dhammapadaṁ seyyo
yaṁ sutvā upasammati.

Should one recite a single word of the Law by hearing which one is at peace, this is better than reciting hundred useless verses.

4. Yo sahassaṁ sahassena
sangāme mānuse jine,
ekañ ca jeyya attānaṁ
sa ve sangāmajuttamo.

Should one man conquer a million men in a battle and another conquer himself, the latter indeed is the greater conqueror.

5. Attā have jitaṁ seyyo
yā cāyaṁ itarā pajā,
attadantassa posassa
niccaṁ saññatacārino.

The conquest of self indeed is better than conquering others. The person who is self-subdued and ever restrained.

6. N'eva devo, na gandhabbo,
na Māro saha Brahmunā,
jitaṁ apajitaṁ kayirā
tathārūpassa jantuno.

Neither a god, nor a demigod (*Gandharva*) nor *Māra* nor *Brahmā* can undo the victory of such a one.

Explanation 5-6

The effects of the victory won by conquering thousands of soldiers in a battle are not abiding, nor unlimited. But the victory of one who conquers self by destroying internal enemies is eternal and beyond limit. Under no circumstances such a victory can be turned into a defeat.

7. Māse māse sahassena
yo yajetha sataṁ samaṁ
ekañ ca bhavitattānaṁ
muhuttam api pūjaye,
sā yeva pūjnā seyyo
yañ ce vassasataṁ hutaṁ.

Though a person may spend in sacrifice one thousand every month for a hundred years, yet should he only honour for a moment a saint who has perfected himself, that honour is better than a century of sacrifice.

8. Yo ce vassasataṁ jantu
aggiṁ paricare vane,
ekaṁ ca bhavitattānaṁ
muhuttam api pūjaye,
sā yeva pūjnā seyyo
yañ ce vassasataṁ hutaṁ.

Though a person may tend the sacrificial fire in the forest for a century yet should he honour only for a moment a saint who has perfected himself, that honour is better than a century of fire worship.

9. Yaṁ kiñci yiṭṭhaṁ va hutaṁ va loke
saṁvaccharaṁ yajetha puññapekho,
sabbampi taṁ na catubhāgam eti
abhivādanā ujjugatesu seyyo.

In this world, for the sake of merit if a person should perform a sacrifice or a fire-worship for a year, all that is not worth one-fourth of the honour paid to the Upright which is better.

10. Abhivādanasīlissa
niccam vaddhāpacāyino
cattāro dhammā vaḍḍhanti:
āyu, vaṇṇo, sukham, balam.

Four things—age, beauty, happiness and strength—increase for him who ever honours and worships the elders.

11. Yo ca vassasataṁ jīve
dussīlo asamāhito,
ekāhaṁ jīvitaṁ seyyo
sīlavantassa jhāyino.

A single day's life of a person who is virtuous and meditative, is better than a hundred years' life of a person who is immoral and of uncomposed mind.

12. Yo ca vassasataṁ jīve
duppañño asamāhito,
ekāhaṁ jīvitaṁ seyyo
paññāvantassa jhāyino.

A single day's life of a person who is wise and meditative, is better than a hundred years' life of a person who is foolish and of uncomposed mind.

13. Yo ca vassasataṁ jīve
kusīto hīnavīrīyo,
ekāhaṁ jīvitam seyyo
viriyam ārabhato daḷhaṁ.

A single day's life of a person who makes strong efforts, is better than a hundred years' life of a person who is slothful and without energy.

14. Yo ca vassasataṁ jīve
apassaṁ udayabhayaṁ,
ekāhaṁ jīvitaṁ seyyo
passato udayabhayaṁ.

A single day's life of a person who sees the rise and fall (of all things), is better than a hundred years' life of a person who does not see them.

15. Yo ca vassasataṁ jīve
apassaṁ amatam padaṁ,
ekāhaṁ jīvitaṁ seyyo
passato amataṁ padaṁ.

A single day's life of a person who sees the Deathless state (*Nibbāna*), is better than a hundred years' life of a person who does not see the Deathless state.

16. Yo ca vassasataṁ jīve
apassaṁ dhammam uttamaṁ,
ekāhaṁ jīvitaṁ seyyo
passato dhammam uttamaṁ.

A single day's life of a person who sees the Sublime Doctrine is better than a hundred years' life of a person who does not see the Sublime Doctrine.

Sahassavaggo Aṭṭhamo

9. PĀPAVAGGA
(EVIL)

1. Abhittharetha kalyāṇe,
pāpā cittaṁ nivāraye;
dandham hi karoto puññaṁ
pāpasmiṁ ramatī mano.

Let one make haste in doing good, let one check one's mind from evil; for if one is slow in doing good one's mind delights in evil.

Explanation 1

One should strive to translate one's good thoughts into action, whenever they occur. Otherwise, the immoral faculties of mind will put them down. One should always resist the onslaught of evil thoughts which debase and defile the mind. The mind of a common man is under the sway of evil propensities which eclipse the noble sentiments. Therefore, the hesitation or delay in doing good deeds may often lead to frustration.

2. Pāpaṁ ce puriso kayirā
na taṁ kayirā punappunaṁ,
na tamhi chandaṁ kayirātha,
dukkho pāpassa uccayo.

If a person commits sin he should not do it again and

again, let him not take a liking for it, for accumulation of evils is painful.

3. Puññaṁ ce puriso kayirā,
kayirātha'etaṁ punappunaṁ,
tamhi chandaṁ kayirātha,
sukho puññassa uccayo.

If a person does a good deed he should do it again and again; let him delight in it, for accumulation of good is blissful.

Explanation 3

Even if a sinful deed is done by mistake, one should be alert that it is not repeated again. For, it brings forth unhappy results. One should not stop doing good by merely doing it once, but go on repeating it again and again. Resultantly one's future will be bright and blissful.

4. Pāpo'pi passati bhadraṁ
yāva pāpaṁ na paccati,
yadā ca paccati pāpaṁ
atha pāpo pāpāni passati.

Even an evil doer sees happiness as long as the evil deed does not mature, but when the evil deed matures, then the evil doer realises evils.

5. Bhadro'pi passati pāpaṁ
yāva bhadraṁ na paccati,

yadā ca paccati bhadraṁ
atha bhadro bhadrāni passati.

Even a good doer sees ill as long as the good deed does not mature; but when the good deed matures then the good doer sees the good.

Explanation 5

Very easy and simple is the doing of sinful deeds. People are allured to do the same for their evanescent ease and happiness. When they indulge therein, they ignore the atrocious consequences thereof. But they come to realise the baneful effects when the bad deeds mature into fruition. On the other hand, the performance of good deeds is difficult. The doer cannot accept the same as blissful in the beginning. But when their blissful results greet him, his happiness knows no bounds.

6. M'āvamaññetha pāpassa
'na maṁ taṁ āgamissati',
udabindu nipātena
udakumbho'pi pūrati,
pūrati bālo pāpassa
thokathokam'pi ācinaṁ.

Do not think lightly of evil, saying, 'It will not come unto me'. Even a water pot is filled by the falling of drops, so the fool fills himself with evil collecting them even little by little.

7. M'āvamaññetha puññassa
'na maṁ taṁ āgamissati',
udabindu nipātena
udakumbho'pi pūrati,
pūrati dhīro puññassa
thokathokam'pi ācinaṁ.

Do not think lightly of good, saying, 'It will not come unto me.' Even as a water pot is filled by the falling of drops, so the wise man collecting even little by little fills himself with good.

8. Vāṇijo'va bhayaṁ maggaṁ
appasattho mahaddhano,
visaṁ jīvitukāmo'va
pāpāni parivajjaye.

Let one avoid evils as does a merchant possessing great wealth, but having a few caravan followers, avoids a way full of danger, or one desirous to live avoids poison.

Explanation 8

While carrying merchandise an unarmed wealthy merchant remains always alert to avoid peril, likewise, in the journey of life one should carefully avoid evils so that internal enemies may not spell ruin.

9. Pāṇimhi ce vaṇo nāssa,
hareyya pāṇinā visaṁ,

nābbaṇaṁ visamanveti,
natthi pāpaṁ akubbato.

If there be no wound in the hand one may carry poison in it. Poison does not affect the unwounded (hand). There is no sin for the person who does not commit evil.

Explanation 9

Even if a sinless holy person comes in contact with the sinner or witnesses the performance of evil deeds, he remains unaffected. For, he has gone beyond the sphere of sins.

10. Yo appaduṭṭhassa narassa dussati
suddhassa posassa anaṅgaṇassa,
tameva bālaṁ pacceti pāpaṁ
sukhumo rajo paṭvātaṁ'va khitto.

The evil falls back on that very fool who offends a harmless, pure and guiltless person, like the fine dust thrown against the wind.

11. Gabbhaṁ eke uppajjanti
nirayaṁ pāpakammino,
saggaṁ sugatino yanti
parinibbanti anāsavā.

Some are born in a womb; and the evil doers are

born in hell. The righteous go to heaven and they who are free from defilements attain *Nibbāna*.

Explanation 11

After death the destination of men does not become the same. In pursuance of the law of *Karma* some take birth in the womb, some are born in hell and some go to heaven. But an emancipated holy person who is beyond the cycle of birth, attains the supreme bliss and peace of *Nibbāna*.

12. Na antalikkhe na samuddamajjhe
    na pabbatānaṁ vivaraṁ pavissa
    na vijjatī so jagatippadeso
    yatthaṭṭhito muñceyya pāpakammā.

Not in the sky, nor in the middle of the ocean, nor having entered a mountain cave, is found that spot in the world where one may escape his evil deeds.

13. Na antalikke na samuddamajjhe
    na pabbatānaṁ vivaraṁ pavissa
    na vijjatī so jagatippadeso
    yatthaṭṭhitaṁ nappasahetha maccu.

Not in the sky, nor in the middle of the ocean, nor having entered the cave of the mountains is found that spot in the world where one may not be overcome by death.

Pāpavaggo Navamo

10. DAṆḌAVAGGA (PUNISHMENT)

1. Sabbe tasanti daṇḍassa
sabbe bhāyanti maccuno,
attānaṁ upamaṁ katvā
na haneyya na ghātaye.

All fear the rod, all are afraid of death. Comparing oneself with others, one should neither kill nor cause to kill.

Explanation 1

"As I am afraid of punishment, fear, death and desire to live, so all others dread punishment, tremble in the name of death and like to cling to life." Realising the fact perfectly one should neither kill nor hurt.

2. Sabbe tasanti daṇḍassa,
sabbesaṁ jīvitaṁ piyaṁ,
attānaṁ upamaṁ katvā
na haneyya na ghātaye.

All fear the rod, life is dear to all. Comparing oneself with others, one should neither kill nor cause to kill.

3. Sukhakāmāni bhūtāni
yo daṇḍena vihiṁsati,

attano sukhaṁ esāno,
pecca so na labhate sukhaṁ.

One who seeking one's own happiness, molests by the rod beings who desire their own happiness, does not get happiness after death.

4. Sukhakāmāni bhūtāni
yo daṇḍena na hiṁsati,
attano sukhaṁ esāno,
pecca so labhate sukhaṁ.

One who seeking one's own happiness, does not molest by the rod beings who desire their own happiness, gets happiness after death.

Explanation 4

Naturally all the beings are after happiness and desire to avoid sufferings. By molesting such happiness-loving creatures even if one gains happiness for the time being, he is bound to suffer hereafter consequently.

One who refrains from molesting others ignoring one's own happiness, will be blessed with peace and happiness hereafter.

5. Mā'voca pharusaṁ kañci,
vuttā paṭivadeyyu taṁ,
dukkhā hi sārambhakathā
paṭidaṇḍā phuseyyu taṁ.

Speak not harshly to anyone, those thus spoken to may retort. Vindictive speech is indeed painful; and blows may be returned to you for blows.

6. Sace heneresi attānaṁ
kaṁso upahato yathā,
esa patto'si nibbānaṁ,
sārambho te na vijjati.

If you silence yourself like a cracked metal gong, you have already attained *Nibbāna*, for there is no retaliation in you.

7. Yathā daṇḍena gopālo
gāvo pāceti gocaraṁ,
evaṁ jarā ca maccū ca
āyuṁ pācenti pāṇinaṁ.

As a cowherd drives his cattle to a grazing ground by a stick, so old age and death drive the life of men (to an end).

8. Atha pāpāni kammāni
karaṁ bālo na bujjhati,
sehi kammehi dummedho
aggidaḍḍho'va tappati.

And yet the fool doing evil deeds does not realise what he does. By his own deeds the stupid man is consumed as if burnt by fire.

9. Yo daṇḍena adaṇḍesu
appaduṭṭhesu dussati,
dasannam aññataraṁ ṭhānaṁ
khippameva nigacchati.

One who offends by the rod those who are non-violent and harmless, soon comes to one of the ten evil states.

10. Vedanaṁ pharusaṁ jāniṁ,
sarirassa ca bhedanaṁ,
garukaṁ vā'pi ābādhaṁ,
cittakkhepaṁ va pāpuṇe.

Either he will be subjected to cruel suffering, a loss, a bodily injury, a serious disease, insanity.

11. Rājato vā upassaggaṁ,
abbhakkhānaṁ va dāruṇaṁ,
parikkhayaṁ va ñātīnaṁ,
bhogānaṁ va pabhaṇguraṁ.

Or oppression from the king, a fearful accusation, a loss of relatives, destruction of wealth.

12. Athav'assa agārāni
aggi ḍahati pāvako,
kāyassa bhedā duppañño
nirayaṁ sopapajjati.

Or his house will be burnt by ravaging fire. And that stupid person will be born in hell after death.

13. Na naggacariyā na jaṭā na paṅkā
nānāsakā thaṇḍilasāyikā vā,
rajo va jallaṁ ukkuṭikappadhānaṁ
sodhenti maccaṁ avitiṇṇakaṅkhaṁ.

Neither wandering naked, nor matted hair, nor dirt, nor fasting, nor lying on the raised ground, nor besmearing the body with dust, nor squatting exertion can purify a mortal who has not overcome his doubts.

14. Alaṅkato ce'pi samaṁ careyya
santo danto niyato brahmacārī
sabbesu bhūtesu nidhāya daṇḍaṁ
so brāhmaṇo, so samaṇo, sa bhikkhu.

Even though a person be gaily adorned, if he should live in peace, calm, restrained, assured (of the right paths), chaste and has set aside rod towards all beings, he is a *Brahmin,* he is an ascetic and he is a *Bhikkhu.*

Explanation 14

The austere performances like wandering naked, squatting on heels, fasting, etc. are mere typical practices. These cannot purify one's mind, nor bring light within. One who controls self, leads a pious life and is tranquil within because of spiritual attainments, is the true sinless sage.

15. Hirīnisedho puriso
koci lokasmiṁ vijjati
yo nindaṁ appabodhati,
asso bhadro kasāmiva.

Such a person is rare indeed in the world who is disciplined by the sense of shame and who would avoid reproach as a well-bred horse avoids the whip.

Explanation 15

[Such sinless, mindful and awakened men are few. They put an end to all sufferings and remain unperturbed among the perturbed.]

—*Saṃyutta Nikāya*

16. Asso yathā bhadro kasāniviṭṭho
ātāpino saṁvegino bhavātha;
saddhāya sīlena ca viriyena ca
samādhinā dhammavinicchayena ca
sampannavijjācaraṇā patissatā
pahassatha dukkhamidaṁ anappakaṁ.

As a good horse touched by the whip, be ye ardent and repentant; rid yourself of this unlimited suffering by being endowed with faith, virtue, energy, concentration, discrimination of the truth, wisdom and good conduct and mindfulness.

17. Udakaṁ hi nayanti nettikā,
usukārā namayanti tejanaṁ,
dāruṁ namayanti tacchakā,
attānaṁ damayanti subbatā.

Irrigators lead the water; fletchers fashion the arrow; carpenters bend wood, those of good practice control themselves.

Daṇḍavaggo Dasamo

11. JARĀVAGGA
(OLD AGE)

1. Ko nu hāso kimānando
niccaṁ pajjalite sati?
andhakārena onaddhā
padīpaṁ na gavessatha?

When the world is ever ablaze what is there to laugh or to be joyous about? Covered by the darkness why do you not seek the light?

Explanation 1

The beings of the world are burnt within and without respectively by the fire of passion, greed, hatred etc. and by that of disease, old age etc. As they are wrapped up by the darkness of ignorance and delusion, they go after pleasures and rejoice over. Be conscious, make an endeavour to get rid of the flames and dispel darkness by seeking light within.

2. Passa cittakataṁ bimbaṁ
arukāyaṁ samussitam
āturaṁ bahusaṅkappaṁ,
yassa natthi dhuvaṁ ṭhiti.

Behold this decorated body a mass of sores, erected (of bones), diseased, variously thought of, and which has no permanent standing.

Explanation 2

When one meditates on the true nature of the body without being charmed by its evanescent beauty, the attachment to body gives way and internal fetters loosen.

3. Parijiṇṇam idaṁ rūpaṁ
roganiḍḍhaṁ pabhaṅguraṁ,
bhijjati pūtisandeho,
maraṇantam hi jīvitam.

This worn-out body a nest of disease is perishable, this foul body breaks up. Indeed, the life ends in death.

4. Yān'imāni apatthāni
alāpūn'eva sārade
kāpotakāni aṭṭhīni
tāni disvāna kā rati?

These pigeon-coloured (dull white) houses are like gourds cast aside in the autumn. What pleasure is there when you see them?

5. Aṭṭhīnam nagaram katam
maṁsalohitalepanaṁ
yattha jarā ca maccū ca
māno makkho ca ohito.

This city wherein decay, death, conceit and hypocrisy are deposited is built of bones and plastered with flesh and blood.

6. Jiranti ve rājarathā sucittā
atho sarīraṁ pi jaram upeti,
satañca dhammo no jaraṁ upeti,
santo have sabbhi pavedayanti.

Indeed gaily decorated royal chariots wear out; so the body also approaches old age; but the teachings of the righteous do not decay. Indeed the good reveal it to the good.

Explanation 6

Although everything in the world decays and disintegrates, but the spiritual culture of the sages never wears out. On the other hand it develops spiritually to lead its adherent to the supreme goal.

7. Appassutāyaṁ puriso
balivaddo'va jīrati:
maṁsāni tassa vaḍḍhanti,
paññā tassa na vaḍḍhati.

The man of little learning grows old like a bull; his flesh increases, but not his wisdom.

8. Anekajātisaṁsāraṁ
sandhāvissaṁ anibbisaṁ
gahakārakaṁ gavesanto,
dukkhājāti punappunaṁ.

Vainly have I wandered for many births, searching for the builder (craving) of this house (body), the birth again and again was painful.

9. Gahakāraka! diṭṭho'si,
puna gehaṁ na kāhasi,
sabbā te phāsukā bhaggā,
gahakūṭaṁ visaṅkhitaṁ,
visaṅkhāragatam cittaṁ,
taṇhānaṁ khayamajjhagā.

O builder of the house! You are seen, You shall build no house again as all your rafters (passions) are broken and the ridge pole (ignorance) is shattered. My mind has attained the unconditioned (*Nibbāna*): it has attained the end of craving.

Explanation 8-9

[The Enlightened One made this solemn utterance under the Bo-tree after his enlightenment.]

Without knowing the causes of birth I wandered through various births which brought forth immeasurable sufferings. However, in the light of Buddhahood I have discovered the unknown. It is the craving which builds this body of flesh and bones. Since it has been destroyed by me with all its accompanying faculties and the ridge pole of ignorance rooted out, there is no more rebirth. My mind is merged in the depth of peace and bliss of *Nibbāna*.

10. Acaritvā brahmacariyaṁ,
aladdhā yobbane dhanaṁ,
jiṇṇakoñcā'va jhāyanṭi
khīṇamacche va pallale.

Men who have not led a holy life and have not earned wealth in the youth, brood like old herons in a pond without fish.

11. Acaritvā brahmacariyaṁ,
aladdhā yobbane dhanaṁ,
senti cāpātikhīṇā'va
purāṇāni anutthunaṁ.

Men who have not led a holy life and have not earned wealth in the youth, lie brooding after the past, like worn-out bows.

Explanation 10-11

Those who neither gained wealth in time, nor engaged themselves in spiritual pursuits by leading a holy life, have to repent in their old age for wasting away life.

Jarāvaggo Ekādasamo

12. ATTAVAGGA
(SELF)

1. Attānaṁ ce piyaṁ jaññā,
takkheyya naṁ surakkhitaṁ;
tiṇṇaṁ aññataraṁ yāmaṁ
paṭijaggeyya paṇḍito.

If oneself is dear to one, one should guard oneself well. The wise man should take care of himself in any of the three watches.

Explanation 1

In the world none can do any harm to or think ill of the dear ones. It is an indisputed fact that self is the dearest of all. But ignorance leads one to bring ruin to self by inducing to indulge in evil thoughts and deeds. This is the advice of the Buddha. One should guard oneself and make one's future happy and blissful by cultivating good during any period of life.

One whose eyes are opened or who sees things in their true perspective, absolves oneself from the grip of evils and marches ahead by purifying the mind by degrees.

2. Attānameva paṭhamaṁ
patīrūpe nivesaye,
ath'aññam anusāseyya,
na kilisseyya paṇḍito.

One should first establish oneself in what is proper; then only he should advise another; such a wise man will not be reproached.

3. Attānaṁ ce tathā kayirā
yathaññam anusāsati,
sudanto vata dammetha,
attā hi kira duddamo.

Let a man do what he teaches another, let him train himself well; for it is really difficult to train oneself.

Explanation 3

It is futile to admonish others to be good and honest without placing the self on the right path. One endowed with self-control finds no difficulty to inspire others with one's own ideal. Attainment of self-control is the problem to be solved.

4. Attā hi attano nātho,
ko hi nātho paro siyā?
attanā'va sudantena
nāthaṁ labhati dullabhaṁ.

For, self is the master of self; who else could be the master? Having trained oneself well, one obtains the best master.

Explanation 4

One whose vision is clouded by the thick veil of ignorance loses oneself in the wilderness of life and gropes helplessly in darkness. To such ones the Buddha's advice is: arise, awake and be a refuge to yourself by thoroughly controlling the self.

5. Attanā'va kataṁ pāpaṁ
attajaṁ attasambhavaṁ,
abhimanthati dummedhaṁ
vajiraṁ vasmamayaṁ maṇīṁ.

The evil done by oneself and originated from oneself, crushes the idiot, like the diamond cuts a crystal stone.

6. Yassa accantadussilyaṁ
māluvā sālamiv'otthataṁ,
karoti so tatha'ttānaṁ,
yathā naṁ icchatī diso.

He, whose evil nature has spread over him as the *Māluvā* creeper over a *Sāl* tree, does unto himself what his enemy wishes him to do.

7. Sukarāni asādhuni
attano ahitāni ca,
yaṁ ve hitañ ca sādhuñ ca,
taṁ ve paramadukkaraṁ.

It is easy to do what is bad and harmful to oneself. That indeed is difficult what is beneficial and good.

8. Yo sāsanaṁ arahataṁ
ariyānaṁ dhammajīvinaṁ,
paṭikkosati dummedho
diṭṭhiṁ nissāya pāpikaṁ
phalāni kaṭṭhakass'eva
attaghaññāya phallati.

The foolish man, who, on account of his evil view, scorns the teaching of the worthy, the noble and the righteous, bears fruits as a bamboo reed for his own destruction.

Explanation 8

When one's misconceptions cloud one's vision and stupefy one, one does not shirk to trifle away the noble teachings of the seers of Truth. Such a person ruins himself only because of his body.

9. Attanā'va kataṁ pāpaṁ
attanā saṅkilissati;
attanā akataṁ pāpaṁ
attanā'va visujjhati;
suddhi asuddhi paccattaṁ
nāñño aññaṁ visodhaye.

The evil done by one defiles oneself; not doing any

evil one purifies oneself. One alone purifies or defiles oneself. One cannot purify another.

Explanation 9

Some ennoble themselves and become great by following in the footsteps of the great, while others degrade and degenerate themselves by adopting evil ways. In fact, the responsibility of ennobling or degrading oneself lies with the self only. In other words, a man himself is responsible for his uplift or downfall and none else.

10. Attadatthaṁ paratthena
bahunā'pi na hāpaye;
attadatthaṁ abhiññāya
sadatthapasuto siyā.

Let one not neglect one's own good on account of others' however great it may be. Let one pursue one's own good knowing it well.

Explanation 10

To do good to others is humanism which deserves praise. However, even for the welfare of others one should not leave the path of one's own spiritual uplift. Under no circumstances one should give up one's meditational practices leading to the realisation of the supreme *Nibbāna.* Otherwise the progress of spiritual development will suffer a setback.

Attavaggo Dvādasamo

13. LOKAVAGGA
(THE WORLD)

1. Hīnaṁ dhammaṁ na seveyya,
pamādena na saṁvase
micchādiṭṭhiṁ na seveyya,
na siyā lokavaddhano.

Let one not follow what is ignoble and let one not dwell in negligence; let one not embrace a wrong view and let one not prolong the world.

Explanation 1

When sensualities, lethargy and misconceptions lead one to an abysmal depth of degradation, one is far away from the path of truth and gets enmeshed in the net of repeated births and deaths. Resultantly one's sufferings know no end. Therefore, the advice of the Compassionate One is: "let not your mind be in the grip of sensual desires, lethargy and misconceptions."

2. Uttiṭṭhe nappamajjeyya,
dhammaṁ sucaritaṁ care,
dhammacārī sukhaṁ seti
asmiṁ loke paramhi ca.

Let one rouse oneself and not be negligent, let one follow the righteous Law thoroughly; the righteous rests happily both in this world and the next.

3. Dhammaṁ care sucaritaṁ,
na naṁ duccaritaṁ care,
dhammacārī sukhaṁ seti
asmiṁ loke paramhi ca.

One should follow the righteous Law thoroughly and not badly; the righteous rests happily both in this world and the next.

Explanation 3

Those who waste away their days of life being in the grip of ignorance and delusion, are deprived of the fine blessings of life and go on extending their sufferings. The advice of the Blessed One to them is: Indulge not in lethargy, listlessness, follow the perfect path of truth so that your life becomes blessed with eternal bliss and peace beyond the reach of all sufferings.

4. Yathā bubbulakaṁ passe,
yathā passe marīcikaṁ,
evaṁ lokaṁ avekkhantaṁ
maccurājā na passati.

The King of death does not see him who views the world as a bubble or a mirage.

Explanation 4

When the light of truth dawns upon one, one views the world and life in their true perspective. He can no longer indulge in delusions over the shadow play, but frees himself from all defilements and goes beyond the cycle of birth and death.

5. Etha passath'imaṁ lokaṁ,
cittaṁ rājarathūpamaṁ,
yattha bālā visīdanti
natthi saṅgo vijānataṁ.

Come I behold world (body), which is like a decked royal chariot, wherein the foolish immerse themselves; but for the wise there is no attachment.

Explanation 5

The external beauty of body which deludes and defiles the mind of a common man, leads him astray. If the nature of the body is seen in its true perspective there is no scope for feeling attraction. In the absence of knowledge anyone feels attracted. But the wise who comprehend the illusive nature of its existence like mirage feel no attraction.

6. Yo ca pubbe pamajjitvā
pacchā so nappamajjati;
so imaṁ lokaṁ pabhāseti,
abbhā mutto'va candimā.

He, who has been negligent before but is vigilant afterwards, illumines this world like the moon emerged from clouds.

7. Yassa pāpaṁ kataṁ kammaṁ
kusalena pithīyati,
so imaṁ lokaṁ pabhāseti,
abbhā mutto'va candimā.

He, whose evil deed is covered by a good deed, illumines this world like the moon emerged from clouds.

Explanation 7

As a man merged in mud washes and cleans himself coming out of it, so one steeped in sins may lead a life of virtue later on and shine amongst men because of it. Such instances are not rare. Ven. Angulimala concerning whom the stanza has been uttered was a notorious man-killer. Once he was a terror to men, but attained the sainthood later on being converted by the Buddha. Hence a sinner may turn a saint by dint of his subsequent spiritual achievements and shine. The sins of such a one are covered by the virtues.

8. Andhabhūto ayaṁ loko
tanuk'ettha vipassati,
sakunto jālamutto'va
appo saggāya gacchati.

The world is blind; a few can see in it. A few go to heaven like a bird freed from the net.

Explanation 8

The people of the world are in the grip of darkness and find no light, their inner eyes being covered by a thick veil of ignorance. A very few of them are blessed with sight, who march towards the supreme goal.

9. Haṁsādiccapathe yanti,
ākāse yanti iddhiyā;
nīyanti dhīrā lokamhā
jetvā māraṁ savāhiṇiṁ.

Swans fly through the sky, those possessed of supernormal powers pass through the air by that power. The wise having conquered the Evil One with his retinue, go across the world to *Nibbāna.*

Explanation 9

Having conquered the internal enemies by means of *sādhanā*—spiritual culture, the wise sages are led beyond the world to enjoy the bliss of emancipation.

10. Ekaṁ dhammaṁ atītassa
musāvādissa jantuno
vitiṇṇaparalokassa
natthi pāpaṁ akāriyaṁ.

There is no evil that cannot be done by him who has transgressed one Law (of truthfulness), who speaks lies and who has given up the (thought of) the next world.

11. Na ve kadariyā devalokaṁ vajanti,
    bālā have nappasaṁsanti dānaṁ,
    dhīro ca dānaṁ anumodamāno,
    teneva so hoti sukhī parattha.

The misers certainly do not go to heaven; indeed foolish do not praise generosity; but the wise man appreciating liberality becomes happy here and hereafter.

12. Pathavyā ekarajjena
    saggassa gamanena vā
    sabbalokādhipaccena
    sotāpattiphalaṁ varaṁ.

The first stage of sainthood is better than the sole sovereignty over the earth or even all the worlds or going to heaven.

Explanation 12

The attainment of *Sotāpatti* which is the first stage of sanctification is a great achievement in life. Nothing can prevent the upward march of the winner of *Sotāpatti*, who must reach the Zenith of realisation of *Nibbāna*. Compared to this state of sainthood all worldly achievements pale into insignificance.

Lokavaggo Terasamo

14. BUDDHAVAGGA
(THE ENLIGHTENED ONE)

1. Yassa jitaṁ nāvajīyati,
jitamassa no yāti koci loke,
taṁ Buddham anantagocaraṁ,
apadaṁ kena padena nessatha?

By what track can you lead Him on a (worldly) way, he who has left no track, the Buddha whose vision is boundless, whose conquest none can undo and whose victory (over passions) none can equal in the world?

2. Yassa jālinī visattikā
taṇhā natthi kuhiñci netave,
taṁ Buddham anantagocaraṁ
apadaṁ kena padena nessatha?

By what track can you lead Him on a (worldly) way, he who has left no track, the Buddha whose vision is boundless, for whom there is no entangling and poisonous craving to lead him anywhere?

3. Ye jhānapasutā dhīrā
nekkhammūpasame ratā,
devāpi tesaṁ pihayanti
sambuddhānaṁ satīmataṁ.

Even the gods long to be like those wise ones who are devoted to meditation, taking delight in the tranquillity of renunciation, mindful and perfectly Enlightened.

4. Kiccho manussapaṭilābho,
kicchaṁ maccāna jīvitaṁ,
kicchaṁ saddhammasavaṇaṁ,
kiccho Buddhānaṁ uppādo.

Difficult it is to be born as a man; difficult is the life of mortals; difficult is the hearing of the Sublime Doctrine; difficult is the appearance of the Buddhas.

Explanation 4

The beasts and birds, insects and the likes bear similarities with men in various respects with only difference in degrees. But unlike men they are deprived of the power of thinking about the goal of life. To make it more clear, they have no conception beyond the sphere of senses. Here lies the supremacy of man who has the scope of development of his latent abilities even to become a superman. Hence the human birth is reckoned as rarity. Rare are the chances of hearing noble teachings which enlighten the mind and that of witnessing the advent of the Buddhas.

5. Sabbapāpassa akaraṇaṁ,
kusalassa upasampadā,
sacittapariyodapanaṁ,
etaṁ Buddhāna sāsanaṁ.

Abstinence from all evil, fulfilment of all good, purification of one's mind is the teaching of the Buddha.

Explanation 5

With a view to reaching the highest goal of life one must shun the path of evils, cultivate good and purify one's mind through spiritual culture—this is the essence of the Buddha teachings.

6. Khantī paramaṁ tapo titikkhā,
nibbānaṁ paramaṁ vadanti Buddhā;
na hi pabbajito parūpaghāti
samaṇo hoti paraṁ viheṭhayanto.

Forbearing patience is the best asceticism; *Nibbāna* is supreme: thus says the Buddha; for one who hurts and molests others is neither a recluse nor a monk.

7. Anūpavādo anūpaghāto,
pātimokkhe ca saṁvaro
mattaññutā ca bhattasmiṁ,
pantaṁ ca sayanāsanaṁ,
adhicitte ca āyogo,
etaṁ Buddhāna sāsanaṁ.

Not blaming, not injuring, strict observance of the *Pātimokkha,* moderation in food, to live in seclusion, devotion to meditation—this is the teaching of the Buddha.

Explanation 7

Indulge not in harmful speech and deed, restrain the self, be moderate in food and earnestly cultivate the meditational practices living in seclusion—this is the advice of the Buddha to those who renounce the world cutting off all ties with the near and dear ones with a view to achieving the supreme goal.

8. Na kahāpaṇa vassena
titti kāmesu vijjati,
appassādā dukhā kāmā
iti viññāya paṇḍito.

There is no satisfaction in sensual pleasures even by a shower of gold coins; sensual pleasures are of little relish and painful; knowing thus, the wise man.

9. Api dibbesu kāmesu
ratiṁ so nādhigacchati,
taṇhakkhayarato hoti
sammāsambuddhasāvako.

Does not find delight even in heavenly pleasures; the disciple of the Fully Enlightened One delights in the destruction of craving.

10. Bahuṁ ve saraṇaṁ yanti
pabbatāni vanāni ca
ārāma rukkha cetyāni
manussā bhayatajjitā.

When threatened by fear men go to many a refuge, to hills, forests, dwellings of ascetics and tree-shrines.

11. Netaṁ kho saraṇam khemaṁ,
netaṁ saraṇam uttamaṁ,
netaṁ saraṇam āgamma
sabbadukkhā pamuccati.

This refuge is not secure indeed, nor it is the supreme refuge, nor having come to this refuge one is freed from all suffering.

12. Yo ca Buddhañ ca Dhammañ ca
Saṅghañ ca saraṇaṁ gato,
cattārī ariyasaccāni
sammappaññāya passati.

He who seeks refuge in the Buddha (Enlightened One), in the *Dhamma* (Doctrine), in the *Saṅgha* (Order), and with the right understanding, sees the Four Noble Truths.

13. Dukkhaṁ dukkhasamuppādaṁ
dukkhassa ca atikkamaṁ
ariyañ c'aṭṭaṅgikaṁ naggaṁ
dukkhūpasamagāminaṁ.

The sorrow, the cause of sorrow, the cessation of sorrow and the Noble Eightfold Path which leads to the cessation of sorrow.

14. Etaṁ kho saraṇaṁ khemaṁ
etaṁ saraṇam uttamaṁ,
etaṁ saraṇam āgamma,
sabbadukkhā pamuccati.

This refuge is secure indeed, this refuge is supreme; having come to this refuge, one is freed from all suffering.

15. Dullabho purisājañño
na so sabbattha jāyati,
yattha so jāyatī dhīro
taṁ kulaṁ sukham edhati.

The thorough-bred man (Buddha) is rare; he is not born everywhere. Where that wise man is born that family attains happiness.

16. Sukho Buddhanaṁ uppādo,
sukhā saddhammadesanā,
sukhā saṅghassa sāmaggī,
samaggānaṁ tapo sukho.

Happy is the appearance of the Buddha; happy is the preaching of the Noble Doctrine; happy is the unity of the Order (*Saṅgha*), happy is the spiritual effort of the United.

17. Pūjārahe pūjayato
Buddhe yadi va sāvake
papañcasamatikkante
tiṇṇasokapariddave.

He who pays homage to those worthy of reverence whether Buddha or his disciples who have crossed over craving, wrong views and conceit, and have overcome grief and lamentation.

18. Te tādise pūjayato
nibbute akutobhaye
nasakkā puññaṁ saṅkhātuṁ
im'ettam iti kena ci.

He who reverences such worthy ones who have attained *Nibbāna* and are free from all fear, his merit cannot be measured by anyone as so much and so much.

Buddhavaggo Cuddasamo

15. SUKKHAVAGGA
(HAPPINESS)

1. Susukhaṁ vata jīvāma
verinesu averino,
verinesu manussesu
viharāma averino.

Ah! happily do we dwell, loving among the hateful; amongst the hateful we live free from hate.

Explanation 1

One who remains unaffected in a society of men poisoned by hatred and ill-will plunges oneself in the bliss of love and purity in such a defiled atmosphere.

2. Susukhaṁ vata jīvāma
āturesu anāturā,
āturesu manussesu
viharāma anāturā.

Ah! happily do we dwell, free from ailments amongst the ailing, amidst the ailing, we live free from ailments.

3. Susukhaṁ vata jīvāma
ussukesu anussukā,
ussukesu manussesu
viharāma anussukā.

Ah! happily do we dwell, free from longing amongst them who long; amidst those who long we live happily without longing.

Explanation 3

Those who are in the grip of sensualism and various sins are led to sufferings. The peace and bliss of the sages who are free from sins and yearn for no sensual pleasure know no bounds.

4. Susukhaṁ vata jīvāma
yasaṁ no natthi kiñcanaṁ,
pītibhakkhā bhavissāma
devā ābhassarā yathā.

Ah! happily do we dwell, having nothing to own; we shall live on joy itself as the radiant gods.

Explanation 4

The sages who are free from fetters of greed, hatred etc. and possess nothing in the world, are verily happy. Like the gods in Radiant heaven who feed on joy, they live a blissful life.

5. Jayaṁ veraṁ pasavati,
dukkhaṁ seti parājito,
upasanto sukhaṁ seti
hitvā jayaparājayaṁ.

The conqueror breeds hatred, the vanquished lie in pain, the peaceful one lies happily, giving up both victory and defeat.

Explanation 5

As the defeat in a battle brings about setbacks and sufferings, so the victory sows the seed of hatred which may develop to create a sense of horror. In one word, both victory and defeat disturb peace and cause harm.

6. Natthi rāgasamo aggi,
natthi dosasamo kali,
natthi khandha samā dukkhā,
natthi santiparaṁ sukhaṁ.

There is no fire like lust, there is no sin like hatred; there is no suffering like the taking up of the five constituents of conditioned existence, no happiness like peace (*Nibbāna*).

Explanation 6

Nothing is so inflammable as lust. It bursts into blaze off and on and burns the mind. Once stirred up, it cannot easily be put down. When hatred seizes, one loses all good senses and can commit the worst of crimes. The living being is nothing but the combination of five aggregates of physical form, of feeling or sensation, of perception, of predisposition and of consciousness. These aggregates bear the existence of a being surrounded by sufferings. Hence no sufferings are like the aggregates or the existence in body and mind. The peace of *Nibbāna* excels all kinds of bliss in as much as the achievement thereof puts an end to all sufferings.

7. Jighacchāparamā rogā,
sankhārā paramā dukhā,
etaṁ ñatvā yathābhūtaṁ
nibbāṇam paramaṁ sukhaṁ.

Hunger is the greatest disease, five aggregates the greatest suffering; knowing this as it really is (the wise should realise) *Nibbāna* the highest bliss.

8. Ārogyaparamā lābhā,
santuṭṭhī paramaṁ dhanaṁ,
vissāsaparamā ñātī,
nibbāṇaṁ paramaṁ sukhaṁ.

Health is the highest gain, contentment the greatest wealth, the trustworthy man is the best relation; *Nibbāna* is the highest bliss.

9. Pavivekarasaṁ pītvā
rasaṁ upasamassa ca
niddaro hoti nippāpo
dhammapītirasaṁ pibaṁ.

Having enjoyed the flavour of solitude and peace, one who imbibes the flavour of the joy of Truth becomes free from fear and sin.

Explanation 9

Having experienced the unspeakable bliss of realisation of *Dhamma* a sinless sage living in a secluded place goes beyond the range of all sorrow and sufferings and remains merged in the depth of peace of *Nibbāna*. He is above all defilements.

10. Sāhu dassanam ariyānaṁ
sannivāso sadā sukho,
adassanena bālānaṁ
niccam eva sukhī siyā.

The seeing of the Noble Ones is auspicious; living with them is ever a happiness. By not seeing fools one would always be happy.

11. Bālasaṅgatacārī hi
dīgham addhāna socati,
dukkho bālchi saṁvāso
amitten'eva sabbadā,
dhīro ca sukhasaṁvāso
ñātīnaṁ'va samāgamo.

For, one who lives in company of fools grieves for a long time; association with fools is always as painful as the association with a foe; association with the wise is as happy as the association with kinsfolk.

12. Tasmā hi,—

Dhīraṁ ca paññañ ca bahussutaṁ ca
dhorayhasīlaṁ vatavantam āriyaṁ
taṁ tādisaṁ sappurisaṁ sumedhaṁ
bhajetha nakkhattapathaṁ'va candimā.

Therefore, follow one who is wise, intelligent, learned, able to lead, dutiful and noble; let one follow such a good and wise one even as the moon follows the path of stars.

Explanation 12

One gets improved morally and spiritually by keeping company with the sinless ones, while the bad association leads one to degradation. Therefore, it is advised that one should improve oneself by following in the footsteps of the wise and virtuous ones.

Sukkhavaggo Paṇṇarasamo

16. PIYAVAGGA (AFFECTIONS)

1. Ayoge yuñjam attānaṁ
yogasmiñ ca ayojayaṁ,
atthaṁ hitvā piyaggāhī
pihet'attānuyoginaṁ.

He who engages himself in what is undesirable and leaves out what is desirable, who grasps the pleasure and abandons the good, envies him who exerts for his good.

Explanation 1

The sensual pleasures appear to be the summum bonum of life to a common man in the grip of delusion. In his mad search for pleasures he indulges in doing wrong and leaves the right path. If the good sense dawns upon him, such a person becomes remorseful and admires one following the right path for spiritual development.

2. Mā piyehi samāgañchi,
appiyehi kudācanaṁ,
piyānaṁ adassanaṁ dukkhaṁ
appiyānañ ca dassanaṁ.

Do not be involved with the beloved, and never with the hated. Not seeing the beloved is sorrowful; and so is the sight of the hated.

3. Tasmā piyaṁ na kayirātha,
piyāpāyo hi pāpako,
ganthā tesaṁ na vijjanti
yesaṁ natthi piyāppiyaṁ.

Therefore have no affection; for the separation from the beloved is painful. To whom there are neither the beloved nor the hated, for them there are no bonds.

Explanation 3

One should live detached leaving both familiarity and dislike. The sufferings caused by either will not befall one in that case. Verily free from fetters are those who are blessed with enlightenment and entertain neither familiarity nor dislike.

4. Piyato jāyatī soko,
piyato jāyatī bhayaṁ,
piyato vippamuttassa
natthi soko, kuto bhayaṁ?

Grief arises from what is dear, fear also does arise from what is dear. One who is wholly free from endearment has no grief, what to speak of fear!

Explanation 4

Generally one desires to resist separation from persons or things of love and affection and remains in constant fear of losing the beloved. If separation or loss occurs in spite of alertness, one's grief knows no bounds. But one who is desireless and detached is beyond the reach of sorrow and fear.

5. Pemato jāyatī soko,
pemato jāyatī bhayaṁ,
pemato vippamuttassa
natthi soko, kuto bhayaṁ?

Grief arises from affection; fear also does arise from affection. One who is wholly free from affection has no grief; what to speak of fear!

6. Ratiyā jāyatī soko,
ratiyā jāyatī bhayaṁ,
ratiyā vippamuttassa
natthi soko, kuto bhayaṁ?

Grief arises from fondness, fear also does arise from fondness. One who is wholly free from fondness has no grief; what to speak of fear!

7. Kāmato jāyatī soko,
kāmato jāyatī bhayaṁ,
kāmato vippamuttassa
natthi soko, kuto bhayaṁ?

Grief arises from lust, fear also does arise from lust. One who is wholly from lust has no grief; what to speak of fear!

8. Taṇhāya jāyatī soko,
taṇhāya jāyatī bhayaṁ,
tanhāya vippamuttassa
natthi soko, kuto bhayaṁ?

Grief arises from craving, fear also does arise from craving. One who is wholly free from craving has no grief; what to speak of fear!

9. Sīla-dassana-sampannaṁ
dhammaṭṭhaṁ saccavedinaṁ
attano kamma kubbānaṁ
taṁ jano kurute piyaṁ.

The people hold him dear who is possessed of virtue and insight, is righteous and truthful, and who fulfils his duties.

Explanation 9

One who places an ideal before the masses by purity of character, clearness of vision, virtuousness, truthfulness and by fulfilment of duties is loved and admired by all.

10. Chandajāto anakkhāte,
manasā ca phuṭo siyā,
kāmesu ca appaṭibaddhacitto,
'Uddhaṁsoto' ti vuccati.

He who aspires after the unspoken (*Nibbāna*) and realises it in his mind, and is detached from lust, is called "One bound upstream".

Explanation 10

Nibbāna which is known through realisation only, cannot be expressed in language. One who developed an earnest desire to reach the supreme goal of *Nibbāna* and experienced the bliss of realisation of stages thereof is beyond the sphere of sensualities and lives unaffected in the world like a lotus in the mud. Such a person is called "upstream bound" (i.e. one destined to attain the supreme *Nibbāna*).

11. Cirappavāsiṁ purisaṁ
dūrato sotthim āgataṁ,
ñātimittā suhajjā ca
abhinandanti sāgataṁ.

Just as relatives, friends and well-wishers welcome a person who has returned safely from a distant place, after a long absence.

12. Tath'eva katapuññam pi
asmā lokā paraṁ gataṁ,
puññāni paṭigaṇhanti
piyaṁ ñātiṁva āgataṁ.

Likewise, he who has done good is received by his good deeds, when he is gone from this world to the next, as relatives receive the dear one on his return.

Piyavaggo Solasamo

17. KODHAVAGGA
(ANGER)

1. Kodhaṁ jahe, vippajaheyya mānaṁ,
saññojanaṁ sabbam atikkameyya,
taṁ nāmarūpasmiṁ asajjamānaṁ
akiñcanaṁ nānupatanti dukkhā.

Let one give up anger, root out egotism and overcome all fetters; sufferings will not overtake him who does not cling to name and form and owns nothing.

Explanation 1

As anger bursts into flame to burn away everything good within, so pride is a stumbling block to one's internal development. One should never entertain these internal enemies but overcome them and get rid of all fetters. A sage who clings to nothing and is free from all fetters, is beyond the reach of all sufferings.

2. Yo ve uppatitaṁ kodhaṁ
rathaṁ bhantam'va dhāraye,
taṁ ahaṁ sārathiṁ brūmi,
rasmiggāho itaro jano.

He who checks his roused anger like a chariot out of its track, him I call a charioteer. The rest of the men are holders of rein.

Explanation 2

As an expert charioteer can regulate rightly the chariot because of his skill in driving, so one who can overcome the inflaming anger is a true controller of self.

3. Akkodhena jine kodhaṁ,
asādhuṁ sādhunā jine,
jine kadariyaṁ dānena,
saccena alikavādinaṁ.

Let one conquer the angry by love, the wicked by good, the stingy by liberality and a lie by truth.

Explanation 3

Anger may be provoked like a sleeping snake on a flimsy ground and cannot be pacified by retaliation which magnifies it only. As a snake is charmed by incantations, so anger may be appeased by the touch of love. Hence the advice of the Lord is to overcome the angry by amity. Goodness is an antidote to wickedness. It is worthwhile to conquer the heart of the wicked by good dealings. One's narrow-mindedness tends to make one stingy. A change of mind may be effected in him by setting examples of liberality. Since a lie gives way to untruthfulness, one should overcome the liar by truthfulness.

4. Saccaṁ bhaṇe, na kujjheyya,
dajjā'ppasmim pi yācito
etehi tīhi ṭhānehi
gacche devāna santike.

Let one speak truth and not be angry; let one give even from the little he possesses to him who begs. By these things one shall go to the company of gods.

5. Ahiṁsakā ye munayo
niccaṁ kāyena saṁvutā
te yanti accutaṁ ṭhānaṁ
yattha gantvā na socare.

Those harmless sages who are ever restrained in body go to the Deathless State, where having gone they never grieve.

6. Sadā jāgaramānānaṁ
ahorattānusikkhinaṁ
nibbāṇaṁ adhimuttānaṁ
atthaṁ gacchanti āsavā.

Defilements fade away of those who are ever awakened, who train themselves day and night and who are bent on *Nibbāna.*

Explanation 6

Those who are awakened by driving out sleepiness view the world in its true perspective. The worldly pleasures cannot therefore allure them. They devote themselves to spiritual pursuits leaving aside worldly matters and keenly desire for the blissful *Nibbāna.* Their internal defilements such as lust, hatred etc. melt away.

7. Porāṇaṁ etaṁ Atula!
n'etaṁ ajjatanām iva,
nindanti tuṇhim āsīnaṁ,
nindanti bahubhāṇinam,
mitabhāṇinam pi nindanti,
natthi loke anindito.

O Atula! this has come from ancient time, this is not a matter of today, they blame him who is silent and him who talks much; also him who talks little. There is none in this world who is not blamed.

8. Na cāhu, naca bhavissati,
na c'etarahi vijjati,
ekantaṁ nindito poso,
ekantaṁ vā pasaṁsito.

There never was, there never will be, nor there is now, a person who is wholly blamed or wholly praised.

Explanation 8

Never there was a person, nor will be, nor exists now, who is absolutely praised or blamed.

9. Yañ ce viññū pasaṁsanti
anuvicca suve suve
acchiddavuttiṁ medhāviṁ
paññāsīlasamāhitaṁ.

If the wise praise, having known day after day, a man who is of flawless character, intelligent, and endowed with wisdom and virtue.

10. Nekkhaṁ jambonadasseva
ko taṁ ninditum arahati?
devāpi taṁ pasaṁsanti,
Brahmuṇāpi pasaṁsito.

Who dares to blame him who is like a coin made of purest gold (*Jambonada*)? He is praised even by gods and also by Brahma.

11. Kāyappakopaṁ rakkheyya,
kāyena saṁvuto siyā,
kāyaduccaritaṁ hitvā
kāyena sucaritaṁ care.

Let one guard against outbursts of bodily actions; let one be restrained in body. Having given up evil deeds, let one be of good behaviour by body.

12. Vacīpakopaṁ rakkheyya,
vācāya saṁvuto siyā,
vacīduccaritaṁ hitvā
vācāya sucaritaṁ care.

Let one guard against the outbursts of speech, let one be restrained in speech. Having given up evil speech, let one be of good speech.

13. Manopakopaṁ rakkheyya,
manasā saṁvuto siyā,
manoduccaritam hitvā
manasā sucaritaṁ care.

Let one guard against the outbursts of the mind, let one be restrained in mind. Having given up evils of the mind, let one be of pure mental actions (or of good conduct in mind).

14. Kāyena saṁvutā dhīrā
atho vācāya saṁvutā
manasā saṁvutā dhīrā
te ve suparisaṁvutā.

The wise who are restrained in body, in speech and in mind are certainly well restrained.

Kodhavaggo Sattarasamo

18. MALAVAGGA
(IMPURITY)

1. Paṇḍupalāso 'va dāni' si
   yamapurisā pi ca taṁ upaṭṭhitā,
   uyyogamukhe ca tiṭṭhasi,
   pātheyyam pi ca te na vijjati.

You are now like a withered leaf; also the messengers of death wait on you; and you are about to depart; there is no provision too with you for the journey.

2. So karohi dīpam attano,
   khippaṁ vāyama, paṇḍito bhava;
   niddhantamalo anaṅgaṇo
   dibbaṁ ariyabhūmim ehisi.

So make an island unto yourself, exert promptly and be a wise man. When your impurities are blown away and you are sinless, you will enter the celestial plane of the Elect.

Explanation 2

What is the good of being dejected and dispirited at the fag end wasting away frivolously the best days of life. Without delay exert yourself hard to ensure the passage for the next world and follow the path of wisdom. Washing away all sins in the stream of *Dhamma* come to the blissful world of sages which is beyond the cycle of birth and death.

3. Upan tavayo va dāni'si,
sampayāto'si Yamassa santike,
vāso pi ca te natthi antarā,
pātheyyam pi ca te na vijjati.

Your life is now drawn to a close; you have come to the presence of death; and there is no halting place for you on the way; also there is no provision with you for the journey.

4. So karohi dīpam attano,
khippaṁ vāyama, paṇḍito bhava;
niddhantamalo anaṅgaṇo
na puna jātijaraṁ upehisi.

So make an island unto yourself, exert promptly and be wise. When your impurities are blown away and you are sinless, you will not come again to birth and decay.

5. Anupubbena medhāvi
thokathokaṁ khaṇe khaṇe
kammāro rajatass'eva
niddhame malam attano.

The wise man should purge himself of impurities, little by little, moment after moment, as a smith removes the dross of silver.

Explanation 5

The mind is full of impurities like envy, hatred, greed, conceit, etc. The wise man endeavours every moment to blot out the same gradually little by little in order to make the mind bright and beautiful.

6. Ayasā'va malaṁ samuṭṭhitaṁ,
taduṭṭhāya tam eva khādati,
evaṁ atidhonacārinaṁ
sakakammāni nayanti duggatiṁ.

As the rust sprung from iron corrodes the same, having arisen from it, so the transgressor is led to evil state by his own deeds.

7. Asajjhāyamalā mantā,
anuṭṭhānamalā gharā,
malaṁ vaṇṇassa kosajjam,
pamādo rakkhato malaṁ.

Non-recitation is the taint of hymns, neglect is the taint of houses, laziness is the taint of beauty; negligence is the taint of a protector.

8. Mal'itthiyā duccaritaṁ,
maccheraṁ dadato malaṁ,
malā ve pāpakā dhammā
asmiṁ loke paramhi ca.

Misconduct is the taint of a woman; avarice is the taint of a benefactor. Indeed! evil deeds are taints both in this world and the next.

9. Tato malā malataraṁ
avijjā paramaṁ malaṁ,
etaṁ malaṁ pahatvāna
nimmalā hotha bhikkhavo.

Of all the taints ignorance is the worst, it is the greatest taint. O *Bhikkhus*! abandoning this taint, be taintless.

Explanation 7-9

Lack of cultivation of the scriptures is a taint because one's proficiency in them suffers on that ground. Non-exertion is the taint of homes, their prosperity being dependent on exertion. As sloth stands in the way of taking proper care of body, it leads to the loss of physical beauty. Carelessness constitutes a drawback of watchman. Bad character ruins a woman. Niggardiness prevents a donor from being generous. Similarly, evils darken both the worlds. Hence, all these are taints in their respective spheres. The worst of all taints is ignorance which leads one to an abysmal depth of degradation. Hence, the Lord exhorts the seekers after truth to get rid of it and be taintless.

10. Sujīvaṁ ahirikena
kākasūrena dhaṁsinā

pakkhandinā pagabbhena
saṅkiliṭṭhena jīvitaṁ.

The life is easy to live for him who is shameless, impudent as a crow, belittling others, bold, arrogant and corrupt.

11. Hirimatā ca dujjīvaṁ
niccaṁ sucigavesinā
alīnen'appagabbhena
suddhājīvena passatā.

The life is hard for him who is modest, who seeks purity always, who is alert, humble, pure in livelihood and who is a seer.

12. Yo pāṇam atipāteti,
musāvādañ ca bhāsati,
loke adinnaṁ ādiyati,
paradārañ ca gacchati.

Whoever in the world takes life, speaks untruth, steals and commits adultery.

13. Surāmerayapānañ ca
yo naro anuyuñjati,
idh'evameso lokasmiṁ
mūlaṁ khaṇati attano.

And a man who is addicted to intoxicating drinks digs up his own roots in this very world.

14. Evam bho purisa, jānāhi
pāpadhammā asaññatā,
mā taṁ lobho adhammo ca
ciraṁ dukkāya randhayuṁ.

Know thus O good man! that such are the unrestrained wicked thoughts, let not greed and wickedness drag you to prolonged suffering.

15. Dadā ti ve yathāsaddhaṁ
yathā pasādanaṁ jano,
tattha yo maṅku bhavati
paresaṁ pānabhojane,
na so divā vā rattiṁ vā
samādhiṁ adhigacchati.

People give according to their faith and devotion. Whoever shrinks when food and drink are given to others, does not get concentration either by day or by night.

16. Yassa c'etaṁ samucchinnaṁ
mūlaghaccaṁ samūhataṁ,
sa ve divā vā rattiṁ vā
samādhiṁ adhigacchati.

He indeed, in whom this (envy) is fully cut off,

uprooted and destroyed, gets concentration by day and night.

17. Natthi rāgasamo aggi,
natthi dosasamo gaho,
natthi mohasamaṁ jālaṁ,
natthi taṇhāsamā nadī.

There is no fire like lust, there is no grip like hatred, there is no net like delusion, there is no river like craving.

Explanation 17

More intense is the burning of lust within than that of fire. It cannot be pacified easily. Similarly, the grip of hatred is worse than that of the wild animal.

The wild animal can tear one to pieces once only, but hatred goes on playing havoc with one repeatedly life after life. Hardest is the net of delusion, since one can hardly proceed towards the world of bliss by getting rid of it. However strong may be the current, a river can be crossed, but insurmountable is the difficulty of overcoming craving within, caught in the current of which the beings suffer without end.

18. Sudassaṁ vajjaṁ aññesaṁ,
attano pana duddasaṁ,
paresaṁ hi so vajjāni
opuṇāti yathābhusaṁ;
attano pana chādeti
kaliṁ'va kitavā saṭho.

Others' fault is easily seen, but it is hard to see one's own. One winnows others' faults like chaff, but covers one's own like a cunning man hides (his) unlucky die from the other gambler.

19. Paravajjānupassissa
niccaṁ ujjhānasaññino
āsavā tassa vaḍḍhanti,
ācā so āsavakkhayā.

He who sees the fault of others and is always criticising, his defilements grow; he is far from the destruction of defilements.

20. Ākāse padaṁ natthi,
samaṇo natthi bāhire
papañcā bhiratā pajā,
nippapañcā Tathāgatā.

There is no track in the sky; no (true) monk is found outside (this order), mankind takes delight in multiplication of wants, Buddhas are free from multiplication of wants.

Explanation 20

As there is no track in the void vault of heaven, so there cannot be a saint outside the domain of spiritual attainments. The masses are in the grip of desires and egotism. But the perfect ones are free from desires and egotism.

21. Ākāse padaṁ natthi,

samaṇo ṇatthi bāhire,

saṅkhārā sassatā natthi,

natthi Buddhānam iñjitaṁ.

There is no track in the sky; no (true) monk is found outside (this order), there are no things that are eternal; and there is no vacillation in Buddhas.

Explanation 21

All things conditioned are impermanent and subject to decay. As the Buddhists are fearless and free from fetters, they waver not.

Malavaggo Aṭṭhārasamo

19. DHAMMAṬṬHAVAGGA (THE MAN OF PRINCIPLE)

1. Na tena hoti dhammaṭṭho
yen'atthaṁ sahasā naye,
yo ca atthaṁ anatthañ ca
ubho niccheyya paṇḍito.

One who gives his decision arbitrarily is not a judge thereby. The wise man having investigated into both, the right and the wrong.

2. Asāhasena dhammena
samena nayatī pare,
dhammassa gutto, medhāvī
dhammaṭṭho'ti pavuccati.

Decides thoughtfully, righteously and impartially, that intelligent person protected by the Law is called a Judge.

3. Na tena paṇḍito hoti
yāvatā bahu bhāsati,
khemī averi abhayo
paṇḍito'ti pavuccati.

One does not become wise because one speaks much, he who is patient, loving and fearless, is called a wise man.

4. Na tāvatā dhammadharo
yāvatā bahu bhāsati,
yo ca appam pi sutvāna
dhammaṁ kāyena passati,
sa ve dhammadharo hoti
yo dhammaṁ nappamajjati.

One is not versed in religious texts (*Dhamma*), because one speaks much. He who realises it mentally after hearing even a little and not negligent of it is indeed well versed in the *Dhamma*.

5. Na tena thero hoti
yen'assa palitaṁ siro,
paripakko vayo tassa
moghajjiṇṇo'ti vuccati.

A man does not become an Elder merely because his head is grey, only his age is ripe, and he is called "grown old in vain".

6. Yamhi saccañ ca dhammo ca
ahiṁsā saññamo damo,
sa ve vantamalo dhīro
thero iti pavuccati.

In whom truth, righteousness, non-violence, restraint and self-control are found, that wise man who has cast off impurity is indeed called an 'Elder'.

7. Na vākkaraṇamattena
vaṇṇapokkharatāya vā
sādhurūpo naro hoti
issukī maccharī saṭho.

One does not become a good man either by mere pleasant talk or by fair complexion, if he is envious, jealous and deceitful.

8. Yassa cetaṁ samucchinnaṁ
sūlaghaccaṁ samūhataṁ,
sa vantadoso medhāvī
sādhurūpo'ti vuccati.

In whom all these are wholly cut off, uprooted and extinct, and who has cast off hatred, that wise man is called good.

9. Na muṇḍakena samaṇo,
abbato alikaṁ bhaṇaṁ;
icchālobhasamāpanno
samaṇo kiṁ bhavissati?

One who does not keep one's vows and speaks lies does not become a monk, by shaving his head. How can one be an ascetic who is full of desire and greed?

10. Yo ca sameti pāpāni
anuṁ thūlāni sabbaso,

samitattā hi pāpānaṁ
samaṇo'ti pavuccati.

He who subdues all evils whether small or great, is called an ascetic, because he has subdued all evils.

11. Na tena bhikkhu hoti
yāvatā bhikkhate pare;
vissaṁ dhammaṁ samādāya
bhikkhu hoti na tāvatā.

One does not become a monk merely because one begs from others, one who observes evil practices does not become a monk on that account.

12. Yo'dha puññañ ca pāpañ ca
bāhetvā brahmacariyavā
saṅkhāya loke carati,
sa ve bhikkhū'ti vuccati.

He, who in this world, having abandoned both merit and demerit, leads a life of purity, dwells in the world understanding it well, is indeed called a *Bhikkhu.*

13. Na monena munī hoti
mūḷharūpo aviddasu;
yo ca tulaṁ'va paggayha
varamādāya paṇḍito.

One who is dull and ignorant does not become a sage by observing silence. The wise who, as if holding the scales, accepts that alone what is the best.

14. Pāpāni parivajjeti,
sa munī tena so munī,
yo munāti ubho loke
munī tena pavuccati.

And rejects the sins is a sage; for he who measures both the worlds is called a *Muni* (sage) on that account.

15. Na tena ariyo hoti
yena pāṇāni hiṁsati;
ahiṁsā sabbapāṇānaṁ
ariyo'ti pavuccati.

One does not become a Noble (*Ārya*) because one kills living beings. By harmlessness towards all living beings one is called the Noble.

16. Na sīlabbatamattena
bāhusaccena vā puna
athavā samādhi lābhena
vivicca sayanena vā.

Neither by good conduct and practices of purification, nor by much learning, nor by attainment of trances, nor by the life of seclusion.

17. Phusāmi nekkhammasukhaṁ
    aputhujjanasevitaṁ,
    bhikkhu vissāsamāpādi
    appatto āsavakkhayaṁ.

Nor by (knowing) that 'I enjoy the bliss of renunciation not enjoyed by ordinary men' should you, O *Bhikkhu*, rest content, without attaining the extinction of the defilements.

Explanation 16-17

The initial successes in meditational practices in the form of visions of brilliant lights, rapturous feelings etc. are often an obstacle to the path of progress. An aspirant for spiritual achievement who develops a subtle desire therefor and misconstrues the phenomenon for blessings, comes to wrong conclusions that he has been blessed with the achievement of different stages of realisation of *Nibbāna* and nothing remains to be done. In order to make the beginners alert the Lord's advice is: Don't abandon effort, go ahead till you reach the goal by rooting out all mental defilements.

Dhammaṭṭhavaggo Ekunavisatimo

20. MAGGAVAGGA
(THE WAY)

1. Maggān'aṭṭhaṅgiko seṭṭho,
saccānaṁ caturo padā,
virāgo seṭṭho dhammānaṁ,
dipadānañ cakkhumā.

Of all paths the Eightfold Path is the best. Of all truths the Four Noble Truths are the best. Of all states the state of passionlessness (*Nibbāna*) is the best. Of all men the Seer (the Buddha) is the best.

Explanation 1

The Eightfold Path, the constituent parts of which are right views, right aspiration, right speech, right action, right livelihood, right endeavour, right mindfulness and right concentration, is the best of all paths, since it opens the eyes and brings forth the supreme enlightenment. The four noble truths viz. suffering, cause of suffering, cessation of suffering and path leading to the cessation of suffering are the best of all truths, as the realisation thereof brings an end to all sufferings and opens the floodgates of bliss. The blissful *Nibbāna* called as passionlessness being beyond the reach of death and decay is the best of all *Dhammas.* Obviously the seer is the best of men because of his wisdom.

2. Eso va maggo, natth'añño,
dassanassa visuddhiyā,

etamhi tumhe paṭipajjatha,
mārass'etaṁ pamohanaṁ.

For the purity of vision this is the only path; there is none other. You follow this very path. For this confounds the *Māra* (the evil one).

3. Etaṁhi tumhe paṭipannā
dukkhass'antaṁ karissatha,
akkhāto ve mayā maggo
aññāya sallasanthanaṁ.

Following this very path you will put an end to suffering. For I have shown this path, knowing the removal of the point of the arrow.

4. Tumhehi kiccaṁ ātappaṁ
akkhātāro Tathāgatā;
paṭipannā pamokkhanti
jhāyino Mārabandhanā.

You yourselves must make the effort; Buddhas but point out the way. Those who meditate and follow it, will escape the bondage of *Māra* (the evil one).

Explanation 4

The Eightfold Path is the true path for the purity of vision by dissolving the darkness of delusion and ignorance. There is no other way to light. One should, therefore, follow this to put an end to all sufferings. Through experience I tell, 'this roots out the spears of lust, hatred etc. I expounded this path for the benefit of seekers. You are to make efforts. I assure you that those who follow this path will reach the supreme goal of life by cutting all fetters.'

5. Sabbe saṅkhārā aniccā'ti
yadā paññāya passati,
atha nibbindati dukkhe;
esa maggo visuddhiyā.

When one realises with wisdom that all conditioned things are impermanent, one gets disgusted with suffering. This is the Path of Purity.

6. Sabbe saṅkhārā dukkhā'ti
yadā paññāya passati,
atha nibbindati dukkhe;
esa maggo visuddhiyā.

When one realises with wisdom that all things are painful, one gets disgusted with sufferings. This is the Path of Purity.

7. Sabbe dhammā anattā'ti
yadā paññāya passati,
atha nibbindati dukkhe;
esa maggo visuddhiyā.

When one realises with wisdom that all things are substanceless, one gets disgusted with suffering. This is the Path of Purity.

Explanation 5-7

All creations are transient. Just like the bubbles in the running waters everything in the world comes into being only to dissolve away. Such transitory things cannot bring about true happiness, nor can they be accepted as reality identified with Self-Sense of 'I' or 'mine'. Whosoever has realised this, he craves for nothing. The abandonment of cravings is the way to reach the supreme goal of *Nibbāna.*

8. Uṭṭhānakālamhi anuṭṭhahāno
yuvā balī ālasiyaṁ upeto,
saṁsanna saṅkappamano kusīto
paññāya maggaṁ alaso na vindati.

He who is young and strong, but slothful, whose mind is full of inertia and is dull, does not exert when he should, that lazy man will not find the path of wisdom.

9. Vācānurakkhi manasā susaṁvuto,
kāyena ca akusalaṁ na kayirā;
ete tayo kammapathe visodhaye
ārādhaye maggaṁ isippaveditaṁ.

Let one be watchful in speech, well restrained in mind and not do any evil deed through body. Let one purify these three ways of action and win the path taught by the sages.

10. Yogā ve jāyati bhūri,
ayogā bhūrisaṅkhayo;
etaṁ dvedhā pathaṁ ñatvā
bhavāya vibhavāya ca,
tath'attānaṁ niveseyya
yathā bhūri pavaḍḍhati.

Wisdom springs from meditation and decays by lack of it, knowing this twofold path of rise and fall, let one so conduct oneself that wisdom may increase.

Explanation 10

The light of wisdom dawns upon him who engages himself in spiritual pursuits leaving aside worldly pleasure. The more he advances therein, the more develops the wisdom. Thus he reaches the goal. Hence, it is said "wisdom springs from meditation". On the other hand, the darkness of delusion and ignorance wraps up him who seeks after pleasure abandoning meditational practices. Therefore, the Lord's advice is: knowing the opposite ways of advancement and decline one should make an effort to develop wisdom by meditational practices for achievement of the supreme goal.

11. Vanaṁ chindatha mā rukkhaṁ,
vanato jāyati bhayaṁ;
chetvā vanañ ca vanathañ ca
nibbanā hotha bhikkhavo.

O *Bhikkhus*! cut down the forest (lust) not the tree.

Fear arises from the forest. Cutting the forest and the thicket be ye without forest (lust).

Explanation 11

The mind is converted into a forest of evils such as lust, hatred, delusion, envy etc. This forest of evils is as dreadful as the infested forest. The fear of disease, death and decay etc. springs therefrom. Therefore, the Lord advises: "Be free of the forest of evils by destroying it and the woods of lesser evils."

12. Yāvaṁ hi vanatho na chijjati
aṇumatto pi narassa nārisu
paṭibaddhamano va tāva so
vaccho khīrapako va mātari.

For, as long as even a minor thought of lust of man towards women is not severed, so far his mind will be attached as a sucking calf unto its mother.

13. Ucchinda sineham attano
kumudaṁ sāradikaṁ'va pāṇinā;
santimaggam eva brūhaya
nibbāṇaṁ sugatena desitaṁ.

Cut off your craving as one picks up an autumnal lotus with the hand. Cultivate the Path of Peace, the *Nibbāna*, preached by the Blessed One.

Explanation 13

When one bound by attachment moves within the narrow limits of worthy matters, one is far away from the truth and wastes away one's days of life in darkness. Hence, the Lord advises: Cut off your attachment with the hand of meditational practice and cultivate the Noble Eightfold Path with a view to reaching the supreme goal of *Nibbāna* preached by the Auspicious One.

14. Idha vassaṁ vasissāmi
idha hemantagimhisu
iti bālo vicinteti
antarāyaṁ na bujjhati.

Here I shall live in the rainy season and here in the winter and summer. Thus the fool muses and does not realise the hindrances.

15. Taṁ puttapasusammattaṁ
byāsattamanasaṁ naraṁ
su taṁ gāmaṁ mahogho'va
maccu ādāya gacchati.

That man whose mind is intoxicated with attachment to his children and cattle, death seizes and carries him away, as a great flood (washes away) a sleeping village.

16. Na santi puttā tāṇāya
na pitā na'pi bandhavā,

antakenā'dhipannassa
natthi ñātisu tāṅatā.

For him who is overtaken by death, there are neither sons, father nor relatives for protection. For him there is no protection in kinsmen.

17. Etam atthavasaṁ ñatvā
paṇḍito sīlasaṁvuto
nibbānagamanaṁ maggaṁ
khippam eva visodhaye.

The wise man who is restrained by virtue, knowing this fact, should clear immediately the way that leads to *Nibbāna.*

Maggavaggo Visatimo

21. PAKIṆṆAKAVAGGA (THE MISCELLANEOUS)

1. Mattā sukhapariccāgā
passe ce vipulaṁ sukhaṁ,
caje mattā sukhaṁdhīro
sampassaṁ vipulaṁ sukhaṁ.

If a wise man sees abundant happiness in renouncing a little pleasure, let him renounce the little pleasure, keeping the abundant happiness in view.

Explanation 1

Everybody longs after worldly happiness which appears to be the goal of life. Human activities know no end to obtain it. Strictly speaking the worldly happiness is ever deceptive, since it can provide no satisfaction. However, the people cling to it, at the source of real happiness lying within is not known to them. But the worldly happiness holds no charms for a wise one who finds within the real happiness by spiritual pursuits. He gives up the insignificant worldly happiness for the sake of the immense happiness of *Nibbāna.*

2. Paradukkhūpadānena
attano sukhamicchati,
verasaṁsaggasaṁsaṭṭho
verā so na parimuccati.

By inflicting pain on others he who wishes for his own happiness being entangled in the meshes of hatred is never freed from hatred.

Explanation 2

One who causes sufferings to others for one's own happiness, indulges in hateful deeds of killing etc. Such a one entangled in hatred cannot have the peace of mind by getting rid of hatred.

3. Yaṁ hi kiccaṁ tadapaviddhaṁ,
akiccaṁ pana kayirati;
unnaḷānaṁ pamattānaṁ
tesaṁ vaḍḍhanti āsavā.

That which ought to be done is left undone, and that which ought not to be done, is done. Thus the defilements of those that are arrogant and negligent increase.

4. Yesañ ca susamāraddhā
niccaṁ kāyagatā sati,
akiccaṁ te na sevanti
kicce sātaccakārīno,
satānaṁ sampajānānaṁ
atthaṁ gacchanti āsavā.

Those who have practised well the meditation on the body, they do not do what should not be done, but are ever earnest in that what should be done. The defilements of such mindful and constantly aware ones come to an end.

Explanation 4

The monks who indulge in improper things unworthy of a monk, giving up their duties such as controlling of senses and meditational practices, are under the sway of internal enemies i.e. passions etc. Hence, their very purpose of renouncement is defeated. But the monks who follow their duties meticulously refraining from wrongful things and devote themselves to spiritual pursuits being established in moral purity, conquer their internal enemies and march towards the supreme goal of *Nibbāna.*

5. Mātaraṁ pitaraṁ hantvā
rājāno dve ca khattiye
raṭṭhaṁ sānucaraṁ hantvā
anīgho yāti brāhmaṇo.

Having killed mother (craving), father (egotism), and two kings of the warrior caste also having destroyed a country (senses and their objects) with the revenue minister (attachment), a *Brahmin* (*Arahant*) goes ungrieving.

6. Mātaraṁ pitaraṁ hantvā
rājāno dve ca sotthiye
veyyagghapañcamaṁ hantvā
anīgho yāti brāhmaṇo.

Having killed mother, father and the two kings of the priest class also having destroyed the five hindrances, a *Brahmin* goes ungrieving.

Explanation 6

Since craving causes rebirth, it is described here as mother. The father being a matter of pride to sons is represented by pride. The views entertained by men are as dominant as kings among men. Hence, the views of eternalism and nihilism are depicted as dual kings. The kingdom and the subjects are the sense organs and their objects. As the tiger is a hindrance to travellers on the forest path, so the five hindrances like passions etc. hinder the progress of spiritual cultivation. Hence they are shown here as the tiger.

7. Suppabuddhaṁ pabujjhanti
sadā Gotamasāvakā,
yesaṁ divā ca ratto ca
niccaṁ Buddhagatā sati.

The disciples of Gotama, who constantly "recollect the greatness of the Buddha", by day and by night, become fully Enlightened.

8. Suppabuddhaṁ pabujjhanti
sadā Gotamasāvakā,
yesaṁ divā ca ratto ca
niccaṁ Dhammagatā sati.

The disciples of Gotama, who constantly "recollect the greatness of the *Dhamma*", by day and night, become full Enlightened.

9. Suppabuddhaṁ pabujjhanti
sadā Gotamasāvakā,
yesaṁ divā ca ratto ca
niccaṁ Saṅghagatā sati.

The disciples of Gotama, who constantly "recollect the greatness of the *Saṅgha* (Order)", by day and by night, become fully Enlightened.

10. Suppabuddhaṁ pabujjhanti
sadā Gotamasāvakā,
yesaṁ divā ca ratto ca
niccaṁ kāyagatā sati.

The disciples of Gotama, who constantly meditate on the body, by day and by night, become fully Enlightened.

11. Suppabuddhaṁ pabujjhanti
sadā Gotamasāvakā,
yesaṁ divā ca ratto ca
ahiṁsāya rato mano.

The disciples of Gotama, who constantly delight in non-violence, by day and by night, become fully Enlightened.

12. Suppabuddhaṁ pabujjhanti
sadā Gotamasāvakā,
yesaṁ divā ca ratto ca
bhāvanāya'rato mano.

The disciples of Gotama, who constantly delight in meditation, by day and by night, become fully Enlightened.

13. Duppabbajjaṁ durabhiramaṁ,
durāvāsā gharā dukhā,
dukkho samānasaṁvāso,
dukkhānupatitaddhagu;
tasmā na c'addhagū siyā,
na ca dukkhānupatito siyā.

It is difficult to take delight in imperfect renunciation; painful is the life in houses where it is difficult to reside. The association with the unequal is painful. Suffering follows a wanderer. Therefore, let not a man be a wanderer (through births and deaths) and be followed by suffering.

Explanation 13

It is easy to renounce the world and to lead a holy life with a view to achieving the highest attainment. Not a bed of roses is also the household life which is bristled with various trials and tribulations. Painful is to stay with those who are different in habits and temperaments. The repeated births of a being are full of sufferings. The Lord therefore advises: Put an end to rebirth and go beyond all sufferings by realisation of the supreme *Nibbāna.*

14. Saddho sīlena sampanno
yasobhogasamappito
yaṁ yaṁ padesaṁ bhajati
tattha tatth'eva pūjito.

A person who is endowed with faith and virtue obtains fame and wealth and to whatever land he goes, is respected then and there.

15. Dūre santo pakāsenti
Himavanto va pabbato,
asant'ettha na dissanti
ratti khittā yathā sarā.

The good are visible from a distance like the Himalayas. The wicked are not visible like the arrows shot at night.

16. Ekāsanaṁ ekaseyyaṁ
eko caramatandito
eko damayaṁ attānaṁ
vanante ramito siyā.

One who sits alone, rests alone, walks alone, one who is strenuous and is controlled alone, he finds delight in the forest.

Pakiṇṇakavaggo Ekavisatimo

22. NIRAYAVAGGA
(HELL)

1. Ab ūtavādī nirayaṁ upeti
yo c'āpi katvā na karomī'ti c'āha,
ubho pi te pecca samā bhavanti,
nihīnakammā manujā parattha.

The liar goes to hell, also the one who having done says, 'I did not do'. Both these men of low deeds, after death, reach the same evil state in the next world.

2. Kāsāvakaṇṭhā bahavo
pāpadhammā asaññatā
pāpā pāpehi kammehi
nirayaṁ te upapajjare.

There are many sinful men, wicked and unrestrained, who are covered with the yellow robe. They are born in hell on account of their evil deeds.

3. Seyyo ayoguḷo bhutto
tatto aggisikhūpamo,
yañ ce bhuñjeyya dussīlo
raṭṭhapiṇḍaṁ asaññato.

It were better to swallow a red hot and flaming ball of iron than to take alms of the country, while being of evil conduct and unrestrained.

Explanation 3

A monk who forgets his pious mission and leads a life of ease and comfort throwing the monastic virtues to the wind brings his ruin only. He is doomed to be born in hell after death.

4. Cattāri ṭhānāni naro pamatto
āpajjati paradarūpasevī:
apuññalābhaṁ, na nikāmaseyyaṁ,
nindaṁ tatīyaṁ, nirayaṁ catutthaṁ.

Four misfortunes befall a negligent man who commits adultery: acquisition of demerit, loss of comfortable sleep, blame and hell.

5. Apuññalābho ca gati ca pāpikā,
bhītassa bhītāya ratī ca thokikā,
rājā ca daṇḍaṁ garukaṁ paṇeti,
tasmā naro paradāraṁ na seve.

And it begets demerit and leads to an evil state in future. The enjoyment of a frightened man with a frightened woman is trifling; and the king also imposes heavy punishment on him. Therefore, no man should go to another's wife.

6. Kuso yathā duggahīto
hattham evānukantati,
sāmaññaṁ dupparāmaṭṭhaṁ
nirayāy'ūpakaḍḍhati.

Just as a *Kusa*-grass wrongly held in hand cuts the very hand, so the monkhood misused drags one to hell.

7. Yaṁ kiñci sithilaṁ kammaṁ
saṇkiliṭṭhañ ca yaṁ vataṁ
saṇkassaraṁ brahmacariyaṁ
na taṁ hoti mahapphalaṁ.

Any loose act, any corrupt observance, a holy life suspiciously, none of these bear much fruit.

8. Kayirā ce kayirāthenaṁ
daḷham enaṁ parakkame,
sithilo hi paribbājo
bhiyyo ākirate rajaṁ.

If there is anything to be done, do it thoroughly; let him do it strenuously. The loose ascetic scatters dust (of evil) all the more.

Explanation 8

One's failure in the observance of monastic vows does no good, but brings forth consequent sufferings. Doing good and leading a pure life necessitate earnest endeavour and tenacity. No great things can be done by a fussy, frail and timid person.

9. Akataṁ dukkataṁ seyyo,
pacchā tapati dukkataṁ,

katañ ca sukataṁ seyyo
yaṁ katvā nānutappati.

An evil deed is better left undone; for the evil deed torments afterwards. Better done is a good deed which having done, one does not repent later.

10. Nagaraṁ yathā paccantaṁ,
guttaṁ santarabāhiraṁ,
evaṁ gopetha attānaṁ
khaṇo ve mā upaccagā,
khaṇātītā hi socanti
nirayaṁhi samappitā.

Let a man guard himself like a frontier-city guarded within and without. Do not let the moment pass; for those who pass the moments (unguarded) repent being consigned to hell.

Explanation 10

As a ruler carefully guards a border city to prevent attacks of the enemies, so with a view to remaining free from the clutches of internal enemies one should guard oneself by controlling the senses. One should never let slip the rare advantages of having human birth and noble company for the sake of momentary pleasures. In the event of such advantages being well-utilised, the blessings of the blissful state will shower on him. Otherwise, there will be no end to repentance.

11. Alajjitāye lajjanti,
lajjitāye na lajjare,
micchādiṭṭhisamādānā
sattā gacchanti duggatiṁ.

Those beings who feel shame in which they should not, and do not feel shame in which they should, holding wrong views, go to hell.

12. Abhaye ca bhayadassino,
bhaye cābhayadassino,
micchādiṭṭhisamādānā
sattā gacchanti duggatiṁ.

Those beings who see fear in which there is no fear, and see no fear in which there is fear, holding wrong views, go to hell.

13. Avajje vajjadassino,
vajje cāvajjadassino,
micchādiṭṭhisamādānā
sattā gacchanti duggatiṁ.

Those beings who think it to be faulty which is free from fault and see no fault in what is faulty, holding wrong views, go to hell.

14. Vajjañ ca vajjato ñatvā,
avajjañ ca avajjato,
sammādiṭṭhisamādānā,
sattā gacchanti suggatiṁ.

Those beings who know fault as a fault and what is free from fault as free from fault holding right views go to heaven.

Nirayavaggo Bāvīsatimo

23. NĀGAVAGGA
(THE ELEPHANT)

1. Ahaṁ nāgo'va saṇgāme
cāpāto patitaṁ saraṁ
ativākyaṁ titikkhissaṁ,
dussīlo hi bahujjano.

As the elephant in a battlefield endures an arrow shot from a bow I shall endure abusive words, for most people are wicked.

2. Dantaṁ nayanti samitiṁ,
dantaṁ rājābhirūhati,
danto seṭṭho manussesu
yo'tivākyam titikkhati.

It is trained animal that is taken in a procession; it is on a trained animal that a king rides. Among men, he who trains himself and endures abuse is the best.

3. Varaṁ assatarā dantā,
ājānīyā ca sindhavā,
kuñjarā ca mahānāgā,
attadanto tato varaṁ.

The mules are excellent when trained; so also are thoroughbred horses of Sindh and the noble elephants, the tuskers. But one who has trained the self is the best of all.

4. Nahi etehi yānehi
gaccheyya agataṁ disaṁ,
yatha'ttanā sudantena
danto dantena gacchati.

One would never go to the unfrequented realm (*Nibbāna*) by these conveyances, as does a restrained one through the subdued and well-trained mind.

5. Dhanapālako nāma kuñjaro
kaṭukappabhedano dunnivārayo
baddho kabalaṁ na bhuñjati,
sumarati nāgavanassa kuñjaro.

The elephant named Dhanapālaka, which is in rut and is hard to control, being in captivity and it recalls the habitat of elephants.

6. Middhī yadā hoti mahagghaso ca
niddāyitā hoti samparivattasāyī
mahāvarāho'va nivāpapuṭṭho
punappunaṁ gabbham upeti mando.

When a person is slothful, gluttonous, sleepy and as he lies rolls from side to side like a pig nourished on pig's wash—that stupid person is born again and again.

Explanation 6

One who has the vices like excessive eating, drowsiness and indolence, can never reach the highest goal of *Nibbāna* by achieving success in spiritual cultivation.

7. Idaṁ pure cittamacāri cārikaṁ
yenicchakaṁ yatthakāmaṁ yathāsukhaṁ,
tadajj'ahaṁ niggahessāmi yoniso
hatthippabhinnaṁ viya aṇkusaggaho.

This mind formerly went wandering as it liked, where it wished, as it lists. Today I shall control it with attentiveness, as an elephant-driver controls a furious elephant.

Explanation 7

So long as one is away from the noble ones and deprived of the opportunities of hearing the sublime *Dhamma*, one is disposed to follow a wrong way being goaded on by base propensities. But if a person is favoured by the opportunities of coming in contact with the holy sages and gets awakened by the noble teachings, he finds an urge within to seek the truth and is determined to have control over the mind for the purpose. Evidently, this stanza smacks of such a determination.

8. Appamādaratā hotha,
sacittam anurakkhatha,
duggā uddharath'attānaṁ
paṅke satto'va kuñjaro.

Delight in vigilance, guard your mind well. Lift yourself out of difficulties as an elephant sunk in mire gets out.

Explanation 8

In an emphatic voice the Lord admonishes the followers: Awake from slumber; let not your mind sink in sensual pleasure and drag yourself out of the mire of base desires and evil propensities so that you may drink deep in the fountain of bliss of *Nibbāna.*

9. Sace labhetha nipakaṁ sahāya
saddhiṁcaraṁ sādhuvihāridhīraṁ,
abhibhuyya sabbāni parissayāni
careyya ten'attamano satīmā.

If one should find an intelligent friend, a companion, who behaves well and is wise having overcome all dangers, one should live with him delightfully and mindfully.

10. No ce labhetha nipakaṁ sahāyaṁ
saddhiṁcaraṁ sādhuvihāridhīraṁ,
rājā'va raṭṭhaṁ vijitaṁ pahāya
eko care mātaṅg'araññe'va nāgo.

If one cannot find an intelligent friend, a companion, who behaves well and is wise, one should live alone as a king who leaves his conquered country and as *Mātanga* elephant that lives alone in the forest.

11. Ekassa caritaṁ seyyo
natthi bāle sahāyatā,
eko care na ca pāpāni kayirā
appossukko mātaṅg'araññe'va nāgo.

Better it is to live alone, there is no companionship with a fool. Live alone, committing no sin and be free from care like *Mātanga* elephant in the forest.

Explanation 11

The good company is absolutely necessary for advancement of life. If one fails to have company of the good and wise, one should live alone and keep away from sins following the noble ideals.

12. Atthamhi jātamhi sukhā sahāyā,
tuṭṭhi sukhā yā itarītarena,
puññaṁ sukhaṁ jīvitasaṅkhayamhi,
sabbassa dukkhassa sukhaṁ pahāṇaṁ.

It is a happiness to have friends in the time of need. Contentment with whatever (we possess) is a happiness. Merit is a happiness when life comes to an end. Removal of all sorrow is a happiness.

Explanation 12

No doubt blissful are real friendship, contentment with one's lot and the merit acquired at the end of life. But the greatest of all blisses is the end of all sufferings by cutting off all fetters.

13. Sukhā matteyyatā loke
    atho petteyyatā sukhā
    sukhā sāmaññatā loke
    atho brahmaññatā sukhā.

In the world it is a happiness to be reverential towards one's mother, then it is a happiness to be reverential towards one's father. It is happiness to be reverential towards a recluse in the world, then it is a happiness to be reverential towards Noble Ones.

14. Sukhaṁ yāva jarā sīlaṁ
    sukhā saddhā patiṭṭhitā
    sukho paññāya paṭilābho
    pāpānaṁ akaraṇaṁ sukhaṁ.

Happy is the practice of virtue before old age approaches; happy is the faith that is firm; happy is the acquisition of wisdom; and happy is the abstention from evil.

Nāgavaggo Tevīsatimo

24. TAṆHĀVAGGA
(CRAVING)

1. Manujassa pamatta cārino
   taṇhā vaḍḍdhati māluvā viya,
   so plavati hurāhuraṁ
   phalam icchaṁ'va vanasmiṁ vānaro.

To a man who is addicted to careless living craving grows like a *Māluvā* creeper. He runs from life to life as a monkey searching for fruits in the jungle.

Explanation 1

The craving is the fundamental cause of rebirth. When one given to pleasures loses control over oneself, one's craving grows by leaps and bounds and overcomes one completely. Such a one gripped by craving jumps from one rebirth to another and finds no end to it.

2. Yaṁ esā sahatī jammī
   taṅhā loke visattikā
   sokā tassa pavaḍḍhanti
   abhivaṭṭhaṁ'va bīraṇaṁ.

Whosoever in this world is overpowered by this base clinging craving, his sorrows grow like *Birana* grass in rainy season.

3. Yo c'etaṁ sahati jammi
tanhaṁ loke duraccayaṁ
sokā tamhā papatanti
udabindū'va pokkharā.

But whosoever in this world overpowers this craving which is base and difficult to overcome, from him sorrows fall away like water drops from a lotus leaf.

Explanation 3

One who is under the sway of craving, finds no end to sufferings consequent on extension of rebirths. In the endless ocean of birth and death one's sorrow and sufferings are on the increase constantly. But one who conquers craving by dint of spiritual cultivation drinks deep in the fountain of bliss of *Nibbāna* and goes beyond the reach of sorrow.

4. Taṁ vo vadāmi bhaddaṁ vo,
yāvant'ettha samāgatā,
taṇhāya mūlaṁ khaṇatha
usīrattho'va bīraṇaṁ,
mā vo naḷam'va soto'va
Māro bhañji punappunaṁ.

Therefore, I say this good thing unto you all those who have assembled here. Dig out the root of craving, as one digs *Birana* grass for its scented root. Let not *Māra* crush you again and again, as the current crushes a reed.

Explanation 4

The Lord admonishes: As the fragrant substance is obtained by digging out the root of *Birana*, so the highest achievement of life becomes a reality by digging up the root of craving. Hence, root out the craving for the great purpose. Don't fall a victim to internal enemies and suffer.

5. Yathāpi mūle anupaddave daḷhe
chinno'pi rukkho punareva rūhati
evam'pi taṇhānusaye anuhate
nibbattatī dukkham idaṁ punappunaṁ.

Just as a tree springs up again even when cut down, if the roots are uninjured and firm, even so, when the tendencies of craving are not rooted out this suffering springs up again and again.

Explanation 5

An atom of craving remaining undemolished may get intensified under favourable conditions and stand in the way of emancipation. Consequently the cycle of rebirths extends with attendant sufferings.

6. Yassa chattiṁsatī sotā
manāpassavaṇā bhusā
vāhā vahanti duddiṭṭhiṁ
saṅkappā rāganissitā.

That man of wrong views, whose thirtysix strong currents (of craving) flow towards pleasures of senses, is carried away by lustful thoughts.

7. Savanti sabbadhī sotā,
latā ubbhijja tiṭṭhati,
tañ ca disvā lataṁ jātaṁ
mūlaṁ paññāya chindatha.

The currents of craving flow everywhere. The creeper of craving stands sprouting. Seeing the creeper sprung up, cut off its roots with wisdom.

Explanation 7

Whatever one sees or hears or smells or tastes or touches or thinks, one feels attracted towards that, if the sensation is agreeable. The attraction is craving which entangles one's mind as does the creeper a tree. Although the creeper of craving is very firm and formidable, yet it is not undestroyable. The wise free themselves from its clutches and plunge in the depth of peace and bliss. Hence, the Lord's advice is: cut the root of craving with the weapon of wisdom.

8. Saritāni sinchitāni ca
somanassāni bhavanti jantuno,
te sātasitā sukhesino
te ve jātijarūpagā narā.

The remembrances of past loves give pleasure to a being. Such persons depending upon the worldly pleasures and trying to find happiness in them indeed go to birth and decay.

Explanation 8

Beings running after happiness like the deer deluded by mirage fall into the trap of craving and find no end to their rebirths. Consequently various sufferings like sorrow and lamentation, decay and death etc. befall them.

9. Tasināya purakkhatā pajā
parisappanti saso'va bādhito,
saññojanasaṅgasattā
dukkhaṁ upenti punappunaṁ cirāya.

Mankind led by craving runs round and round like a tied hare. They being tied by the fetters come to grief again and again for a long time.

10. Tasiṇāya purakkhatā pajā
parisappanti saso'va bādhito,
tasmā tasiṇaṁ vinodaye
bhikkhu ākaṇkhī virāgamattano.

Mankind led by craving runs round and round like a tied hare. Therefore, let the *Bhikkhu*, who desires his own freedom from passion, discard craving.

11. Yo nibbanatho vanādhimutto
vanamutto vanameva dhāvati,
taṁ puggalameva passatha,
mutto bandhanameva dhāvati.

One who is freed from craving (worldly life) by being disposed to forest life, and having been freed from forest (craving) runs back to craving—behold that very person who being freed once runs back to the bondage again.

12. Na taṁ daḷhaṁ bandhanamāhu dhīrā
yadāyasaṁ dārujaṁ babbajaṁ ca,
sārattarattā maṇikuṇḍalesu,
puttesu dāresu ca yā apekkhā.

The wise do not call a bond strong that is made of iron, wood or *Babbaja*-grass. The attachment for jewels and ornaments, children and wives.

13. Etaṁ daḷhaṁ bandhanamāhu dhīrā
ohārinaṁ sithilaṁ duppamuñcaṁ
etampi chetvāna vajanti dhīrā
anapekkhino kāma sukhaṁ pahāya.

This bond is called the strong bond by the wise which though loose and can be carried away, yet from which it is difficult to escape. Those who are free from desire, cut off even this bond and renounce the world having given up sense pleasures.

Explanation 12-13

One's attachment to one's wife and children and belongings is an internal fetter which is much harder than the fetters like iron chain, rope etc. Although the internal fetter does not affect the physical movements, yet it dominates and degrades one's mind. It is not easy to get rid of it. But the sages enjoy the supreme bliss of emancipation by cutting down these fetters.

14. Ye rāgarattānupatanti sotam
sayaṁ kataṁ makkaṭako va jālaṁ,
etam'pi chetvāna vajanti dhīrā
anapekkhino sabbadukkhaṁ pahāya.

Those who are infatuated with lust fall into the stream (of craving) as a spider in its own web. Those men who are free from longing cut off even this (stream) and go (to *Nibbāna*), abandoning all sufferings.

15. Muñca pure muñca pacchato
majjhe muñca bhavassa pāragū,
sabbattha vimuttamānaso
na puna jātijaraṁ upehisi.

Renounce the past, present and the future, and cross to the further shore. With a mind thus entirely freed, you will not come to birth and decay again.

Explanation 15

There should remain no trace of craving for the past,

present and future. Being free from all cravings, go beyond the ocean of being and bring an end to all sufferings.

16. Vitakkapamathitassa jantuno
tibbarāgassa subhānupassino
bhiyyo taṇhā pavaḍḍhati,
esa kho daḷhaṁ karoti bandhanaṁ.

Craving grows steadily for the person who is crushed by evil thoughts, whose lust is sharp and who sees pleasure (in the body). He indeed makes the bond strong.

17. Vitakkūpasame ca yo rato
asubhaṁ bhāvayati sadā sato,
esa kho vyantikāhiti,
eso checchati Mārabandhanaṁ.

One who delights in quenching evil thoughts and meditates on the impurity of the body, one who is ever mindful, such a one will cut off the bond of *Māra.*

Explanation 17

The cravings of one who is extremely attached to worldly things and given to sensual pleasures, grow by leaps and bounds. Consequently one strengthens one's fetters. But dwindle away the craving of one who gives up worldly thoughts and overcomes attachment by meditating on the true nature of the body. Such a one cuts all fetters and remains absorbed in the bliss of *Nibbāna.*

18. Niṭṭhaṇgato asantāsī
vītataṇho anaṇgano
acchiddi bhavasallāni
antimo'yaṁ samussayo.

He who has reached the goal, is fearless, has destroyed craving, is free from passion and has cut down the darts of rebirth, is holding the last body.

Explanation 18

One who has reached the goal and goes beyond the ocean of being by smashing the internal spears of passions, hatred etc. through *Sādhanā*—spiritual culture, is sinless, fearless and devoid of craving such a one holds a final body by putting an end to rebirth. Hence sufferings befall him no more.

19. Vītataṇho anādāno
niruttipadakovido
akkharānaṁ sannipātaṁ
jaññā pubbaparāni ca,
sa ve antimasārīro
mahāpañño mahāpuriso'ti vuccati.

He who is free from craving and grasping, proficient in the meaning of terms, understands the grouping of letters in their prior and posterior relations, such a man is a bearer of the final body and is called a man of profound wisdom.

Explanation 19

One who is free from all impurities of mind and acquainted with the inmost meaning of the *Dhamma* is undoubtedly a great man of profound wisdom. Such a one puts an end to the inexorable play of birth and death with its attendant ills.

20. Sabbābhibhū sabbavidū hamasmi
sabbesu dhammesu anūpalitto
sabbañjaho taṇhakkhaye vimutto,
sayaṁ abhiññāya kamuddiseyyaṁ?

I have overcome all, I know all, I am unattached to everything; having renounced all I am emancipated by destruction of craving. Thus having comprehended myself, whom shall I call my teacher?

Explanation 20

I am the knower of all conquering the internal enemies. My mind is attached to nothing by abandoning all. Cravings being destroyed I am free. Having achieved realisation myself under the Bo-tree I can point out none as my teacher.

21. Sabbadānaṁ dhammadānaṁ jināti,
sabbaṁ rasaṁ dhammaraso jināti,
sabbaṁ ratiṁ dhammaratī jināti,
taṇhakkhayo sabbadukkhaṁ jināti.

The gift of Truth conquers all other gifts. The flavour of Truth conquers all other flavours. The delight in Truth conquers all other delights. The destruction of craving conquers all sufferings.

Explanation 21

The various material gifts no doubt bring relief to the needy, but the gift of *Dhamma* enables one to be blessed with the attainment of enlightenment. Hence it is the best of all gifts. The flavour of *Dhamma* enlivens one with the feelings of piety and purity and ultimately leads one to immortality. Thus, it excels all other flavours. The delight in all the worldly things pales into insignificance in comparison with that in *Dhamma.* Destruction of cravings by realisation of *Nibbāna* brings an end to all sufferings.

22. Hananti bhogā dummedhaṁ
no ca pāragavesino
bhogatanhāya dummedho
hantī aññe'va attanaṁ.

Wealth ruins the fool, but not those who seek the further shore. The fool ruins himself by craving for wealth (if he were ruining) of others.

Explanation 22

An unwise person gaining wealth loses his head and runs after pleasure madly. Such a person brings his own ruin, being caught in the mesh of craving. So he becomes an enemy to himself. But one who wants to be blessed with the peace of *Nibbāna*, remains unaffected by wealth. Such a one advances towards the supreme goal leaving behind all worldly gains.

23. Tiṇadosāni khettāni,
rāgadosā ayaṁ pajā,
tasmā hi vītarāgesu
dinnaṁ hoti mahapphalaṁ.

Weeds are the bane to the fields, lust is the bane to mankind. Therefore, the gift offered to those who are free from lust, yields much fruit.

24. Tiṇadosāni khettāni,
dosadosā ayaṁ pajā,
tasmā hi vītadosesu
dinnaṁ hoti mahapphalaṁ.

Weeds are the bane to the fields, hatred is the bane to mankind. Therefore, the gift offered to those who are free from hatred, yields much fruit.

25. Tiṇadosāni khettāni,
mohadosā ayaṁ pajā,
tasmā hi vītamohesu
dinnaṁ hoti mahapphalaṁ.

Weeds are the bane to the fields, delusion is the bane to mankind. Therefore, the gift that is offered to those who are free from delusion, yields much fruit.

26. Tiṇadosāni khettāni,
icchādosā ayaṁ pajā,
tasmā hi vigaticchesu
dinnaṁ hoti mahapphalaṁ.

Weeds are the bane to the fields; desire is the bane to mankind. Therefore, the gift that is offered to those who are free from desire, yields much fruit.

Explanation 26

A grass does harm to corn fields, so do passion, hatred etc. to men. Those who are freed from the clutches thereof, are worthy of worship. Hence, offerings to them bear immense fruit.

Taṇhāvaggo Catuvisatimo

25. BHIKKHUVAGGA
(THE ALMSMAN)

1. Cakkhunā saṁvaro sādhu,
sādhu sotena saṁvaro,
ghānena saṁvaro sādhu,
sādhu jivhāya saṁvaro.

The restraint of the eye is good; the restraint of the ear is good; the restraint of the nose is good; and the restraint of the tongue is good.

2. Kāyena saṁvaro sādhu,
sādhu yācāya saṁvaro,
manasā saṁvaro sādhu,
sādhu sabbattha saṁvaro;
sabbattha saṁvuto bhikkhu
sabbadukkhā pamuccati.

The restraint of the body is good; the restraint of the speech is good; the restraint of the mind is good. The monk who is restrained in all ways escapes from all miseries.

3. Hatthasaññato pādasaññato
vācāya saññato saññatuttamo
ajjhattarato samāhito
eko santusito tamāhu bhikkhuṁ.

He indeed is called a *Bhikkhu* who is restrained in hand, feet, speech, who highly restrained (in every way), delights in meditation, composed, solitary and contented.

4. Yo mukhasaññato bhikkhu
mantabhāṇi anuddhato
atthaṁ dhammañ ca dīpeti,
madhuraṁ tassa bhāsitaṁ.

The speech of the monk is verily sweet who is restrained in tongue, wise in speech, nor restless and who explains the meaning and the text.

5. Dhammārāmo dhammarato
dhammaṁ anuvicintayaṁ
dhammaṁ anussaraṁ bhikkhu
saddhammā na parihāyati.

The *Bhikkhu* who abides by the Doctrine, who delights in the Doctrine, who contemplates upon the Doctrine and who remembers the Doctrine, does not fall off from the sublime Doctrine.

Explanation 5

The *Bhikkhu* who gets the flavour of *Dhamma,* advances dauntlessly towards the goal. Nothing can stand in his way. He never deviates from the path.

6. Salābhaṁ nātimaññeyya,
nāññesaṁ pihayaṁ care,
aññesaṁ pihayaṁ bhikkhu
samādhiṁ nādhigacchati.

Let not a monk despise his own gain and let him not envy (the gain) of others. The monk who envies (the gain) of others, does not attain concentration.

7. Appalābho'pi ce bhikkhu
salābhaṁ nātimaññati,
taṁ ve devā pasaṁsanti
suddhājīviṁ atanditaṁ.

If a monk does not despise his own gain though it be little, gods praise him indeed, for his livelihood is pure and he is not slothful.

Explanation 7

The *Bhikkhu* who worries over the food and drink given by the laity is far away from moral and spiritual development and the very purpose of his *Bhikkhu*-hood is defeated. The *Bhikkhu* who does not bother about these matters and leads a pure life remaining contented with his own lot advances in his spiritual pursuits. He is praised by all.

8. Sabbaso nāmarūpasmiṁ
yassa natthi mamāyitaṁ,

asatā ca na socati,
sa ve bhikkhū'ti vuccati.

He who does not consider in any way name and form as 'mine' and grieves not, because it is not reality, he indeed is called a monk.

Explanation 8

One who has no ego-sense (i.e. of 'I' and 'mine' in respect of physical and mental existence), no attachment thereto and no grief over disintegration of body and mind i.e. natural decay and death etc. is a true *Bhikkhu.*

9. Mettāvihāri yo bhikkhu
pasanno Buddhasāsane
adhigacche padaṁ santaṁ
saṇkhārūpasamaṁ sukhaṁ.

The monk who contemplates upon universal love (*Metta*), and delights in the teachings of the Buddha, attains that Blissful State of Peace, the cessation of all conditioned things.

Explanation 9

The *Bhikkhu* who is devoted to the cultivation of loving kindness towards all living beings and delighted in following the great ideals of Buddha's teachings merges himself in the depth of peace and bliss of *Nibbāna.*

10. Siñca bhikkhu imaṁ nāvaṁ,
sittā te lahumessati,
chetvā rāgañ ca dosañ ca
tato nibbānamehisi.

O monk! empty this boat of water. Thus emptied it will be easy for you to proceed on. You will go to *Nibbāna* thereby, cutting out lust and hatred.

11. Pañca chinde pañca jahe,
pañca ca uttari bhāvaye,
pañca saṅgātigo bhikkhu
oghatiṇṇo'ti vuccati.

Cut off five (bonds), give up the other five and cultivate five more. The monk who has gone beyond the five associates, is called "one who has crossed the flood".

12. Jhāya bhikkhu! mā ca pamādo,
mā te kāmaguṇe bhamassu cittaṁ,
mā lohaguḷaṁ giḷī pamatto,
mā kandi dukkhamidan'tidayhamāno.

Meditate O monk! Do not be negligent. Do not let your mind whirl on sensual pleasures. Being negligent do not swallow a ball of red-hot iron, and while burning, do not cry "this is suffering".

Explanation 12

This is the Buddha's admonition to the *Bhikkhu.* Leave aside sleepiness and devote yourself to the cultivation of meditational practices to reach the supreme goal. Let not your mind indulge in sensual thoughts and don't swallow the red-hot iron ball of enjoying gifts of the laity as a *Bhikkhu* devoid of virtues and self-restraint. Consequently weep not jumping into the flame.

13. Natthi jhānaṁ apaññassa,
paññā natthi ajhāyato,
yamhi jhānañ ca paññañ ca
sa ve nibbānasantike.

There is no meditation for him who has no wisdom, and there is no wisdom in him who does not meditate. In whom there are both meditation and wisdom, he indeed is nearer to *Nibbāna.*

Explanation 13

One on whom the light of wisdom has not dawned cannot find an access to the realm of concentration by defeating the onslaught of internal enemies—passion, hatred, etc. One who is devoid of concentration cannot be blessed with the divine wisdom. One who possesses both concentration and wisdom reaches the supreme goal of *Nibbāna* leaving behind the worldly play of going and coming.

14. Suññāgāraṁ paviṭṭhassa
santacittassa bhikkhuno,
amānusī ratī hoti
sammā dhammaṁ vipassato.

The monk who has retired to a lonely abode, whose mind is calmed, who perceives things clearly, experiences a joy that is superhuman.

15. Yato yato sammasati
khandhānaṁ udayabhayaṁ,
labhati pītipāmojjaṁ
amataṁ taṁ vijānataṁ.

As much as he reflects on the rise and fall of aggregates, he experiences joy and happiness. This is immortality to those who know.

Explanation 15

When a *Bhikkhu* in a secluded place with peaceful surroundings meditates on the characteristics of impermanence, sorrowful and egolessness in respect of the physical and mental phenomena, an unspeakable joy floods his mind. Everything in the world appears to him just like bubbles in the running waters that arise and dissolve. What is impermanent is nothing but suffering to him and what is suffering is not worth accepting 'I' or 'mine'. The process of this meditation itself is deathlessness to him who knows it.

16. Tattāyaṁ ādi bhavati
idha paññassa bhikkhuno,
indriyagutti santuṭṭhī,
pātimokkhe ca saṁvaro,
mitte bhajassu kalyāṇe,
suddhājīve atandite.

Here in this doctrine it is the start for a wise *Bhikkhu*: guarding senses, contentment, observance of (*Pātimokkha*) precepts with care, and he would associate with beneficent friends who are energetic and pure in livelihood.

17. Paṭisanthāravutyassa,
ācārakusalo siyā,
tato pāmojjabahulo
dukkhass'antaṁ karissati.

He would be cordial and civil in behaviour. Thereby full of joy, he will put an end to suffering.

18. Vassikā viya pupphām
maddavām pamuñcati,
evaṁ rāgañ ca dosañ ca
vippamuñcetha bhikkhavo.

O monks! As the jasmine drops its flowers that are withered away, so drop away lust and hatred.

19. Santakāyo santavāco
santavā susamāhito
vantalokāmiso bhikkhu
upasantoti vuccati.

The monk who is calm in body, calm in speech, calm in mind and well composed and who has renounced worldly gains, is called one tranquillised.

Explanation 19

The mind of a *Bhikkhu*, who is serene and tranquil in body, speech and mind by destroying delusion, lust etc. and cutting off all internal fetters, remains merged in the depth of peace of *Nibbāna.*

20. Attanā coday'attānaṁ,
paṭimāse attaṁ attanā,
so attagutto satimā
sukhaṁ bhikkhu vihāhisi.

O *Bhikkhu*! censure your 'self' by 'yourself', examine your 'self' by 'yourself'. Then self-guarded and mindful you will live happily.

21. Attā hi attano nātho,
attā hi attano gati,
tasmā saññamay'attānaṁ
assaṁ bhadram'va vāṇijo.

Self indeed is the refuge of self; for self is (the maker of) one's own future life. Therefore, control your 'self' as a merchant controls a horse of noble breed.

Explanation 21

The Lord admonishes: O *Bhikkhu*, you depend on none for self-advancement, but look within, awake and be mindful. As you are the lord of yourself, control your own self, place yourself on the right path and march ahead towards the supreme goal.

22. Pāmojjabahulo bhikkhu
pasanno Buddhasāsane
adhigacche padaṁ santaṁ
sankhārūpasamaṁ sukhaṁ.

A monk full of joy, and has faith in the Doctrine of the Buddha will attain the peaceful state, the ending of conditioned things, the bliss.

23. Yo have daharo bhikkhu
yuñjati Buddhasāsane
so imaṁ lokaṁ pabhāseti
abbhā mutto'va candimā.

The young monk who devotes himself to the teaching of the Buddha, he indeed illumines this world like the moon freed from a cloud.

Explanation 23

Even if a *Bhikkhu* young in age follows perfectly the teachings of the Buddha, he reaches the height of spiritual attainments and shines in glory of bright virtues and wisdom amongst men.

Bhikkhuvaggo Pañcavīsatimo

26. BRĀHMAṆAVAGGA (THE BRAHMINS)

1. Chinda sotaṁ parakkamma,
kāme panuda brāhmaṇa,
saṅkhārānaṁ khayaṁ ñatvā
akataññū'si brāhmaṇa.

O *Brahmin*! exert and cut off the stream (of craving), discard sensual pleasures. Knowing the destruction of all conditioned things, be one who knows the 'Uncreated One' (*Nibbāna*).

Explanation 1

Cut off the stream of desires which flow within and exterminate the last trace of lust with right effort. Reach the supreme goal of *Nibbāna* (which is unborn and uncreated) by realising the characteristics of impermanence in respect of all created things appearing in their true colours.

2. Yadā dvayesu dhammesu
pāragū hoti brāhmaṇo,
ath'assa sabbe saṁyogā
atthaṁ gacchanti jānato.

When the *Brahmin* has fully accomplished the two (concentration and insight), then all fetters of that knowledgeable one disappear.

3. Yassa pāraṁ apāraṁ vā
pārāpāraṁ na vijjati,
vitaddaraṁ visaṁyuttaṁ,
tamahaṁ brūmi brāhmaṇaṁ.

For whom there is neither this shore nor that shore (six internal senses and external objects) not both together, who is undisturbed and is free from attachment, him I call a *Brahmin.*

Explanation 3

Undistressed and fetterless is one who is not perturbed by the concept of "I" and "mine", being freed from fetters through spiritual culture and who does not suffer from the sense of duality (i.e. the perception of 'I' and 'you') in the absence of ego-sense. Such a person is the real *Brahmin.*

4. Jhāyiṁ virajam āsīnaṁ
katakiccaṁ anāsavaṁ,
uttamatthaṁ anuppattam
tamahaṁ brūmi brāhmaṇaṁ.

He who is meditative, stainless, settled, has done his duty, is free from defilements and has attained the highest goal, him I call a *Brahmin.*

5. Divā tapati ādicco,
rattiṁ ābhāti candimā,

sannaddho khattiyo tapati,
jhāyī tapati brāhmaṇo,
atha sabbaṁ ahorattiṁ
Buddho tapati tejasā.

The sun shines by day; the moon shines by night, the warrior shines in armour, the *Brahmin* shines in meditation. But the Buddha shines whole day and night by his glory.

6. Bāhitapāpo'ti brāhmaṇo,
samacatiyā samaṇo'ti vuccati,
pabbājay'attano malaṁ,
tasmā pabbajito'ti vuccati.

Because one has banished evils, one is called a *Brahmin,* and one is called a monk (*Samaṇa*) by just conduct. Because one has discarded one's impurities, therefore one is called a recluse (*Pabbajita*).

7. Na brāhmaṇassa pahareyya,
nāssa muñcetha brāhmaṇo,
dhī brāhmaṇassa hamāraṁ,
tato dhī yassa muñcati.

Let none strike a *Brahmin* and a *Brahmin* should not show ill-will to one who strikes. Shame on him who strikes a *Brahmin,* more shame on him who expresses ill-will to one who strikes.

8. Na brāhmaṇass'etadakiñci seyyo
yadā nisedho manaso piyehi
yato yato hiṁsamano nivattati
tato tato sammatimeva dukkhaṁ.

Refraining from (retaliation) which is dear to one's mind, is of no small advantage to a *Brahmin.* As much as one averts one's mind from violence so much one's sorrow subsides.

9. Yassa kāyena vācāya
manasā natthi dukkataṁ
saṁvutaṁ tīhi ṭhānehi
tamahaṁ brūmi brāhmaṇaṁ.

He who does not do evil deeds through body, speech or mind, he who is restrained in these three ways, him I call a *Brahmin.*

10. Yamhā dhammaṁ vijāneyya
sammāsambuddhadesitaṁ
sakkaccaṁ taṃ namasseyya
aggihuttaṁ'va brāhmaṇo.

Through whomsoever one should learn the Law preached by the Fully Enlightened One, one should bow to him with reverence as a *Brahmin* (reveres) the sacrificial fire.

Explanation 10

One should be devoted and respectful to whosoever enlightens one on the aspects of *Dhamma* or shows the way to realisation of *Nibbāna.*

11. Na jaṭāhi na gottena
na jaccā hoti brāhmaṇo,
yamhi saccañ ca dhammo ca
so sucī so ca brāhmaṇo.

Neither by matted hair nor by clan nor by birth does one become a *Brahmin.* But in whom there exist both truth and piety he is the pure and is the *Brahmin.*

12. Kiṁ te jaṭāhi dummedha!
kiṁ te ajinasāṭiyā
abbhantaraṁ te gahaṇaṁ
bāhiraṁ parimajjasi?

Of what use is your matted hair? O wicked man! of what use is your deer skin? Within you there is a thicket (of passion), you merely clean outwardly.

Explanation 12

One gains nothing by mere putting on the garb of a recluse. The outward refinement leads one nowhere, while evil thoughts thrive within.

13. Paṁsukūladharaṁ jantuṁ
kisaṁ dhamanisanthataṁ,
ekaṁ vanasmiṁ jhāyantaṁ
tamahaṁ brūmi brāhmaṇaṁ.

The person who wears a robe made of rags, who is lean, who is emaciated, who meditates alone in the forest, him I call a *Brahmin.*

Explanation 13

A real *Brahmin* is he who covers his body with robes collected from the road leaving aside luxury and meditates in the forest being contented with food just required for maintenance of the body having no greediness for food-stuff.

14. Na cāhaṁ brāhmaṇaṁ brūmi
yonijaṁ mattisambhavaṁ,
bhovādi nāma so hoti
sa ce hoti sakiñcano,
akiñcanaṁ anādānaṁ
tamahaṁ brūmi brāhmaṇaṁ.

Him I do not call a *Brahmin* who is born from the womb of a mother. He may be addressed merely as 'Sir' if he is well-to-do. He who is free from any possession and is not grasping, him I call a *Brahmin.*

15. Sabbasaññojanaṁ chetvā
yo ve na paritassati,
saṅgātigaṁ visaṁyuttaṁ
tamahaṁ brūmi brāhmaṇaṁ.

Having cut off all fetters he who verily fears not, he who has left behind all bonds and is detached from the world, him I call a *Brahmin.*

16. Chetvā naddhiṁ varattañ ca
sandāmaṁ sahanukkamaṁ,
ukkhittapaḷighaṁ Buddhaṁ
tamahaṁ brūmi brāhmaṇaṁ.

He who having cut off the strap (hatred), the thong (craving) and the rope (heresies) with all that pertains to it (latent tendencies), has removed the obstacles (Ignorance), and is enlightened, him I call a *Brahmin.*

17. Akkosaṁ vadhabandhañ ca
aduṭṭho yo titikkhati,
khantibalaṁ balānīkaṁ
tamahaṁ brūmi brāhmaṇaṁ.

He who endures reviling, flogging and imprisonment without resentment, whose army is the power of patience, him I call a *Brahmin.*

18. Akkodhanaṁ vatavantaṁ
sīlavantaṁ anussutaṁ
dantaṁ antimasārīraṁ
tamahaṁ brūmi brāhmaṇaṁ.

He who is free from anger, dutiful, virtuous, is without attachment, restrained and is bearing his final body, him I call a *Brahmin.*

Explanation 18

One endowed with vows and virtues, who has destroyed desires and anger and gone beyond the cycle of birth and death to bear the last body by reaching the zenith of spiritual enlightenments is the real *Brahmin.*

19. Vāri pokkharapatte'va
āraggeriva sāsapo,
yo na limpati kāmesu
tamahaṁ brūmi brāhmaṇaṁ.

As water on a lotus leaf, or a mustard seed on the point of an awl, he who does not cling to sensual pleasures, him I call a *Brahmin.*

20. Yo dukkhassa pajānāti
idh'eva khayamattano,
pannabhāraṁ visaṁyuttaṁ
tamahaṁ brūmi brāhmaṇaṁ.

Having laid the burden aside and being detached, from the world, who realises the destruction of his suffering in this very life, him I call a *Brahmin.*

21. Gambhīrapaññaṁ medhāviṁ
maggāmaggassa kovidaṁ,
uttamatthaṁ anuppattaṁ
tamahaṁ brūmi brāhmaṇaṁ.

He who possesses profound knowledge, who is wise, who knows the right and wrong way and who has attained the supreme goal, him I call a *Brahmin.*

22. Asaṁsaṭṭhaṁ gahaṭṭhehi
anāgārchi cūbhayaṁ
anokasāriṁ appicchaṁ
tamahaṁ brūmi brāhmaṇaṁ.

He who does not get mixed with both laymen and mendicants, he who is homeless, and whose wants are few, him I call a *Brahmin.*

23. Nidhāya daṇḍaṁ bhūtesu
tasesu thāvaresu ca
yo na hanti na ghāteti,
tamahaṁ brūmi brāhmaṇaṁ.

He who has laid aside the rod towards beings whether moving or still, he who neither slays nor causes to slay, him I call a *Brahmin.*

24. Aviruddhaṁ viruddhesu
attadaṇdesu nibbutaṁ
sādānesu anādānaṁ
tamahaṁ brūmi brāhmaṇaṁ.

He who is friendly among the hostile, peaceful among those who wield the rod, is free from grasping among those who are grasping, him I call a *Brahmin.*

25. Yassa rāgo ca doso ca
māno makkho ca pātito
sāsaporiva āraggā
tamahaṁ brūmi brāhmaṇaṁ.

From whom lust, ill-will, conceit and envy have fallen off, like a mustard grain (that slips off) from the point of an awl, him I call a *Brahmin.*

26. Akakkasaṁ viññāpaṇiṁ
giraṁ saccaṁ udīraye
yāya nābhisaje kaṇel
tamahaṁ brūmi brāhmaṇaṁ.

He who speaks gentle, instructive and true words, and whose words do not offend anyone, him I call a *Brahmin.*

Explanation 26

One who realises the Supreme *Nibbāna* being fully

enlightened frees himself from the fear of undergoing afflictions of rebirth by breaking off all fetters.

27. Yo'dha dīghaṁ va rassaṁ vā
aṇuṁ thūlam subhāsubhaṁ
loke adinnaṁ nādiyati
tamahaṁ brūmi brāhmaṇaṁ.

In the world, he who does not steal anything, either long or short, small or great, good or bad, him I call a *Brahmin.*

28. Āsā yassa na vijjanti
asmiṁ loke paramhi ca
nirāsayaṁ visaṁyuttaṁ
tamahaṁ brūmi brahmaṇaṁ.

Who has got no expectations for this world or for the next, he who is desireless and unattached, him I call a *Brahmin.*

29. Yassālayā na vijjanti
aññāya akathaṅkathī,
amatogadhaṁ anuppattaṁ
tamahaṁ brūmi brāhmaṇaṁ.

He who has no craving, having understood (the truth), who is freed from doubts, and has merged into the Deathless (*Nibbāna*), him I call a *Brahmin.*

30. Yo'dha puññañ ca pāpañ ca
ubho saṅgaṁ upaccagā
asokaṁ virajaṁ suddhaṁ
tamahaṁ brūmi brāhmaṇaṁ.

In the world, who has left off attachment for both good and evil, he who is free from sorrow, and stain, and is pure, him I call a *Brahmin.*

31. Candaṁ'va vimalaṁ suddhaṁ
vippasannam anāvilaṁ
nandībhavaparikkhiṇam
tamahaṁ brūmi brāhmaṇaṁ.

He who is clean and pure like the moon, is sinless and undisturbed, he who has destroyed craving for becoming, him I call a *Brahmin.*

32. Yo imaṁ palipathaṁ duggaṁ
saṁsāraṁ mohamaccagā,
tiṇṇo pāragato jhāyi
anejo akathaṅkathī,
anupādāya nibbuto
tamahaṁ brūmi brāhmaṇaṁ.

He who has crossed over this difficult miry path, this circle of births and deaths and delusion, having crossed has reached the other shore, he who is meditative, free from craving and doubt, grasping nothing has attained *Nibbāna,* him I call a *Brahmin.*

Explanation 32

One who has, by means of steady cultivation of meditational practices, crossed the deluding and difficult worldly existence defiled by lust and hatred etc. and infested with evils, is merged in the peace of blissful *Nibbāna.* Such a person is the true *Brāhmin.*

33. Yo'dha kāme pahatvāna
anāgāro paribbaje
kāma-bhavaparikkhīṇaṁ
tamahaṁ brūmi brāhmaṇaṁ.

In this world, he who having given up sensual pleasures renounces home and becomes a homeless one, he who has destroyed lust and becoming, him I call a *Brahmin.*

34. Yo'dha taṇhaṁ pahatvāna
anāgāro paribbaje,
taṇhā-bhavaparikkhīṇaṁ
tamahaṁ brūmi brāhmaṇaṁ.

In this world, he who having given up craving renounces home and becomes a homeless one, he who has destroyed craving and becoming, him I call a *Brahmin.*

35. Hitvā mānusakaṁ yogaṁ
dibbaṁ yogaṁ upaccagā,
sabbayogavisaṁyuttaṁ
tamahaṁ brūmi brāhmaṇaṁ.

He who having left behind human bonds has transcended heavenly bonds, he who is completely detached from all bonds, him I call a *Brahmin.*

Explanation 35

One who is completely emancipated from all ties, craving neither for human pleasures nor for heavenly happiness is a true *Brahmin.*

36. Hitvā ratiñ ca aratiñ ca
sītibhūtaṁ nirūpadhiṁ,
sabbalokābhibhuṁ vīraṁ,
tamahaṁ brūmi brāhmaṇaṁ.

He who has given up both enjoyment and discontentment, who is cooled and is without belongings, is a hero that has conquered the whole world, him I call a *Brahmin.*

37. Cutiṁ yo vedi sattānaṁ
upapattiñ ca sabbaso,
asattaṁ sugataṁ Buddhaṁ,
tamahaṁ brūmi brāhmaṇaṁ.

He who in every way knows the death and rebirth of beings, who is free from attachment, well gone and enlightened, him I call a *Brahmin.*

38. Yassa gatiṁ na jānanti
devā gandhabbamānusā,
khīṇāsavaṁ arahantaṁ,
tamahaṁ brūmi brāhmaṇaṁ.

He whose future state is not known either by the gods or Gandharvas or men, he who has destroyed all defilements and is an *Arahant*, him I call a *Brahmin.*

Explanation 38

None can see the goal of one who has reached the highest peak of attainments and become a sinless one by demolishing all defilements. Such a one is the true *Brahmin.*

39. Yassa pure ca pacchā ca
majjhe ca natthi kiñcanaṁ,
akiñcaṇaṁ anādānaṁ,
tamahaṁ brūmi brāhmaṇaṁ.

He who has no clinging to the past, future or present, he who possesses nothing and grasps nothing, him I call a *Brahmin.*

40. Usabhaṁ pavaraṁ vīraṁ
mahesiṁ vijitāvinaṁ
anejaṁ nahātakaṁ Buddhaṁ
tamahaṁ brūmi brāhmaṇaṁ.

He who is a leader, a noble, a hero, a great sage, a conqueror, a desireless one, who has washed away his sins and is enlightened, him I call a *Brahmin.*

41. Pubbe-nivāsaṁ yo vedi
saggāpāyañ ca passati,
atho jātikkhayaṁ patto,
abhiññā vosito muni,
sabbavositavosānaṁ,
tamahaṁ brūmi brāhmaṇaṁ.

He who knows his previous births, he who sees heaven and hell, he who has reached the end of births, a sage who has perfected himself in knowledge and has reached his goal, him I call a *Brahmin.*

Explanation 41

A true *Brahmin* is he who may view events of previous lives like the reflections of things in the mirror, sees things beyond the range of normal vision by supernormal eyes, is beyond birth and death by destroying desires, reached the zenith of holy life through super-knowledge and left no duties undone.

Brāhmaṇavaggo Chabbīsatimo

SOME SAYINGS OF THE BUDDHA FROM THE DHAMMAPADA

The *Dhammapada*, meaning footprints of Law, is a part of the *Sutta-pitaka*. It is an anthology and used as a guidebook for those who pledge themselves to walk in the Way of *Dhamma*. It is in verse and there are four hundred twentythree stanzas composed in various metres. The Commentary on the *Dhammapada*, *Atthakatha*, is supposed to have been written by Buddhaghosa in the first half of the fifth century A.D. "In explaining the verses, he gives for every or nearly every verse a parable to illustrate its meaning, which is likewise believed to have been uttered by the Buddha in his intercourse with his disciples, or in preaching to the multitudes that came to hear him" (Max Muller). There is no reason to doubt that most of the verses, even if they do not reproduce the exact utterances of the Buddha, are true to the spirit of his teachings.

"All that we are, is the result of what we have thought; it is founded on our thoughts, it is made up of our thoughts. If a man speaks or acts with impure thoughts, sorrow follows him, as the wheel follows the foot of the draught animal that draws the carriage. "He abused me, he beat me, he defeated me"—in those who harbour such thoughts hatred will never cease. For hatred does not cease by hatred at any time; hatred ceases by love. This is an eternal law."

"Therefore, overcome the angry by gentleness; the wicked by kindness, the miser by liberality, the liar by truth."

"He who lives without passionate craving for sensuous pleasures, his senses well controlled, moderate in his food, faithful and strong, him the Temper will certainly not overthrow, anymore than the wind throws down a rocky mountain."

"This mind of mine went formerly wandering about as it liked; but I shall now control it thoroughly, as the rider who holds the hook controls the furious elephant. Be not careless! Watch your thoughts! Draw yourself out of the evil way; as an elephant does who is sunk in mud."

"As when a house-roof is not properly secured, the rain finds a way through it and drops within, so when the thoughts are not carefully controlled, the carnal desires will soon bore through all our good resolutions. But as when a roof is well stopped then the water cannot leak through, so by controlling one's thoughts, and acting with reflection, no such desires can arise or disturb us."

When the Buddha was residing at Sravasti, in the Jetavana, there was a young *Bhikkhu*, who being overcome by foolish thoughts was unable to restrain his desires. Grieved at this he resolved to dismember himself, and for that purpose, he went to the house of his patron (*dānapati*), and having procured a knife he proceeded to his cell and sitting on his couch he began to reflect on the evil which resulted from the power of gratifying desire. Buddha knowing his thoughts, and perceiving him to be deceived by ignorance of the true cause of his conduct, an ill-restrained mind, proceeded to his cell, and enquired what he was going to do. On this *Bhikkhu* explained that as he was unable to check desire, and in consequence to advance in religious exercise, he was about to dismember himself. On this the Buddha explained that uncertainty and doubt were the cause of delay in religious progress, that the first thing to do was to govern the mind and restrain the thoughts, without which merely to get rid of the external instrument of evil was useless.

"Not by matted locks, nor by lineage, nor by caste is one a *Brahmin,* he is the *Brahmin* in whom are truth and righteousness and purity. What boots your tangled hair, O fool, what avails your garment of skins? You have adorned the outer parts, within you are full of uncleanliness. Not him do I call a *Brahmin* who is merely born of a *Brahmin* mother, men may give him salutation as a *Brahmin,* though he be not detached from the world; but him I call a *Brahmin* who has attachment to nothing. Him I call a *Brahmin,* indeed, who has cut all fetters, who never trembles, is independent and unshackled. Him I call a *Brahmin,* indeed, who, though he has committed no offence, endures reproach, bonds, and stripes, who has endurance for his force and strength for his army."

When the Buddha was residing in the Jetavana Vihara, at Sravasti, there were four newly-admitted mendicants who went together and sat under a plum-tree, intending to engage themselves in religious contemplation (*dhyāna*). At this time the tree was in full bloom, and struck by the beautiful colours and the fragrant perfume of the blossoms, the conversation of the mendicants took the following turn viz. as to what in all the world was most worthy of love as a source of pleasure. Then one of them said, "I think the greatest happiness in the world is during some moonlit night in spring, when all the trees are in bloom, to wander forth in the country, and take one's pleasure without constraint." Another said, "I think the highest pleasure is in joining in some family social gathering, and enjoying the feast and the wine, the music and the dancing." Another said, "I think the highest happiness is to possess such funds of wealth as to enable one to procure whatever the heart desires, whether it be chariots or horses, clothing or ornaments, such as would make one, on going into the world, the admiration and envy of all beholders." The fourth said, "And I think the highest happiness to be to possess a wife as beautiful as possible, and to see her clad in all the choicest robes, anointed with the rarest unguents, and always ready for the indulgence of love."

Now the Buddha, perceiving that these men were capable of conversion, but had not yet arrived at a knowledge of the impermanency of the six objects of desire, immediately, with a sigh, addressed the four men, and asked them, "What is the subject of your discourse, as you sit here together beneath this tree?" On this they told him truthfully what each one's idea of happiness was. And then the Buddha rejoined, "Let there be an end of such discourse, for all these things (which you desire) are the causes of (way of) sorrow, fear and calamity. This is not the way of eternal peace, the system of the highest joy. The flowers of spring shall fade in autumn and fall in utter decay before the winter cold.

"All those friends in whose society you place such reliance for happiness, ere long shall be scattered and separated far and wide. That wealth you prize and that beauty of wife, and those pleasures, alas! are the causes of every misfortune—hatred in families, wreck of body, future misery! Wherefore, O *Bhikkhus*! be sure that the highest bliss is to search after supreme wisdom, to covet a condition of non-attachment, to desire nought for one's self, to aim at *Nirvāṇa.*" And then the Buddha uttered the following verse:

"From lust comes sorrow, from lust comes fear; where there is no lust, or no ground for lust, what sorrow, what fear can there be? From pleasure comes sorrow, from pleasure comes fear; where there is no ground for pleasure, what grief or fear can there be? From covetousness (greed) comes sorrow, from greed comes fear; where one is free from covetousness, there can be no sorrow or fear. But to be greedy to fulfil perfectly the requirements (moral rules) of the Law—to be truthful in everything, to conduct his own business (to order himself) according to what is right—this is to lay a foundation of love for all. The idea of pleasure not yet produced, his thoughts and words composed, his mind unaffected by any bewilderment of love, he indeed shall mount above or cut off the stream."

"As a tree, as long as its root is firm and safe, although cut down, still survives and produces fruit; so, unless the remnants of lust are destroyed and uprooted, a man must return again and again to receive sorrow. The monkey, away from the tree, first of all enjoys release, and then returns again to its bondage, such is the case with men, they escape from hell and then return to it. Longing thoughts are like the everflowing waters of a river, giving way to the free enjoyment of indolence and luxury, the mind like a savage dog seeks for continual indulgence, and the man himself becomes clouded and unable to see the truth. Every thought flowing in the same channel, then lusts bind a man as with strong rattan bonds. The wise man alone is able rightly to distinguish the truth, he is able to cut off the very root and source of his lustful thoughts. A man by self-indulgence becomes sleek and shining, his thoughts increase like the sprouting tendril, the depth of lust cannot be fathomed; from this proceeds the ever-increasing succession of old age and continual death."

"Neither much learning, nor sacrifices to the Gods, nor sleeping on the ground, nor difficult and strenuous vigils, nor the repetition of prayers, can bring purification to the man enmeshed in delusion. Neither gifts to the priests, nor self-castigation, nor the performance of rites and ceremonies can work purification to him who is filled with craving."

He whom no craving with its snares and poisons can lead astray, by what track can you lead him, the Enlightened? Even the gods envy those who are awakened and mindful, who are given to meditation and who delight in the peace of emancipation from craving.

To refrain from all evil, to achieve good deeds and to purify one's own mind—this is the teaching of the Awakened.

The best of ways is the Eightfold—there is no other that leads to purity of vision (insight). Follow this way and make an end of your suffering. He who does not rouse himself when it is time to rise, who though young and strong, is full of sloth, whose will and thought are weak, that lazy and idle man will never find the way to wisdom.

Watching his speech, well restrained in mind, let a man never commit any wrong with his body, let a man but keep those roads of action clear.

If a man finds a prudent companion to walk with, one who is upright and lives soberly, he may walk with him, but if a man finds no prudent companion to walk with, let him walk alone like a king who has renounced the country he has conquered. It is better to live alone, there is no companionship with a fool.

If one man conquers in battle a thousand men, and if another conquers himself, he is the greatest of conquerors. One's own self conquered is better than the conquest of all other people; not even a god could change into defeat the victory of a man who is self-controlled and always calm.

The *Bhikkhu,* who adheres to the strict rules of a religious life, who guards and controls all his senses, takes his food in moderation, sleeps according to necessity, by these rules subduing his mind, keeping his thoughts in close subjection, inwardly enlightened by wisdom and meditation, never forsaking the right path of enlightenment: thus inwardly illumined, observing the rules of right conduct, satisfied as to the character of true wisdom, proceeding onward in the path of daily duty, this man, at rest in himself, shall get rid of all sorrow.

There was once a man who had no brothers, but only one little son, who was much loved by both his parents. They procured for him means of instruction and fondly hoped that he would be an honour to their house. But, alas! he was careless and negligent, and learned nothing. In consequence of this his parents took him to their home and hoped he would be useful in the management of the house. But he was idle and dirty in his ways, and altogether a grief to them. In consequence of this he was slighted by all the neighbours, and became an object of contempt amongst his friends, and almost hateful to his parents. Deeply touched by this, he sought some comfort in religious exercises, but found no help in all his penances and prayers to the gods. At last, hearing that the Buddha was the all-wise Teacher who could meet the necessities of his case, he came to him and begged his help. To whom the Buddha replied, "If you would find comfort in my society, the first thing for you to learn is purity of conduct. Go back, therefore, to your home, and learn to obey your parents, recite your prayers, be diligent in your daily occupations, let no love of ease tempt you to neglect cleanliness of person or decency of dress; and then, having learned this, come back to me, and you may perhaps be allowed to enter into the companionship of my followers." And then the Buddha spoke as follows:

"Absence of daily prayers is the disease of daily conversation (words). Want of diligence is the disease of a household. Want of becoming dignity is the disease of manner (outward appearance). Carelessness is the disease of business. Stinginess is the disease of charity. Vice is the disease of daily conduct. Both now and hereafter an evil mode of life (law) is an everlasting disease (taint). But the disease of all diseases, than which none is worse, is ignorance."

When the Buddha was residing at Sravasti, there were five hundred *Brahmins* who continuously sought to bring some railing accusation against him. The Buddha, by his divine sight, penetrating their intention, and being moved by compassion towards them, desired to bring them to a knowledge of the truth. They had arranged between themselves to persuade a butcher to ask the Buddha to receive his hospitality, and then, whilst he was there, to cause the slaughter of different creatures around him, so that in condemning slaughter, he must of necessity condemn his host, or in praising his host, he must condone the slaughter. Then the Buddha, having accepted his host's invitation, addressed him thus: "When the fruit is ripe it will fall of itself, so when merit is ripe, it will exhibit of itself (produce salvation)." Then the butcher, returning to his house, made all necessary preparations for the entertainment. At the appointed time the Buddha arrived and addressed the *Brahmins* and those assembled with them:

"The teaching of the wise is this, that by wisdom we preserve ourselves. The foolish ridicule it—they see, and yet do wickedly, and so by their wicked deeds they reap misfortune, as he who sows the noxious plant reaps the same. The wicked man in his own person accumulates (receives the fruit of his) guilt; the good man reaps good fruit (merit) in his own person, and so each one for himself prepares the harvest for himself. The concerns of another do not affect one's case—doing good, then we reap good, just as one who sows that which is sweet enjoys the same."

SELECT BIBLIOGRAPHY

BOOKS

Bapat, P.V. (ed.), *Two Thousand Five Hundred Years of Buddhism*, Delhi 1959

Barua, Beni Madhab, *Gaya and Bodh Gaya—Early History of the Holy Land*, 2 Vols., Calcutta, 1924

Barua, D.K., *Buddha Gaya Temple: Its History*, Buddha Gaya, 1981

Bhattacharya, Tarapada, *The Bodh Gaya Temple*, Calcutta, 1966

Brahmachari, Silananda, *The Eternal Message of Lord Buddha (A Study of Dhammapada)*, Bodh Gaya, 1981

Brough, John (ed.), *The Gandhari Dhammapada*, London, 1962

Carter, J.R. and Palihawadana, Mahinda, *Buddhism: The Dhammapada*, New York, 1992

Chin, Nan Huai, *Basic Buddhism—Exploring Buddhism and Zen*, Mumbai, 2003

Cunningham, A., *Maha Bodhi or the Great Buddhist Temple under the Bodhi Tree at Buddha Gaya*, Delhi (Reprint)

Dhammajoti, Bhikkhu, *The Chinese Version of the Dhammapada*, University of Kelaniya, Sri Lanka, 1995

Dharma Rakshita, Bhikkhu, *Dhammapada*, Benares, 1953

Gangulee, N., *The Buddha and His Message*, Bombay, 1959

Kosambi, Dharmananda, *Bhagavana Buddha*, New Delhi, 1956

Lal, R.B., *Bodh Gaya: Past and Present*, Patna, 1953

Mahathera, Rastrapala, *The Glory of Buddha Gaya*, Shillong, 1967

Mitra, R.L., *Buddha Gaya: The Great Buddhist Temple*, The Hermitage of Sakya Muni, Delhi (Reprint), 1972

Mitra, Swati (Editor and Publisher), *Walking with the Buddha—Buddhist Pilgrimages in India*, New Delhi, 1997

Norman, K.R., *The Word of the Doctrine* (*Dhammapada*), Oxford, 1997

Roy, Prafulla Chandra, *Buddha Vachanamṛta—Dhammapada kā Hindi Kāvyānuvāda*, Bodh Gaya, 1981

Samadar, J.N., *The Glories of Magadha*, Patna, 1924

Sangharakshita, *Dhammapada—The Way of Truth*, Birmingham, 2001

——, *The Eternal Legacy*, Tharpa, London, 1985

Sparham, Gareth, *The Tibetan Dhammapada*, London, 1983

Tagore, Rabindra Nath, *Buddhadeva*, Calcutta, 1902

Valisinha, Deva Priya, *A Guide to Bodh Gaya*, Calcutta, 1960

Vijayatunga, J., *Bodh Gaya*, Delhi, 1956

JOURNALS AND PROCEEDINGS

Buddha Vandana—Buddha Mahotsava, Gaya

The Maha Bodhi—Calcutta

Prajñā—Bodh Gaya

Proceedings of the International Buddhist Conference of the Japanese Temple, Bodh Gaya